No Gout Pain Cookbook

100+ Gout Relief Recipes

Nutritionist Reviewed and Approved

Great Tasting, Low Purine Recipes for People with Gout

3rd Edition
Diane Sanders

Table of Contents

Introduction, ...7

Appetizers & Main Course 8

  Moist Chili Chicken 8

  Fish Tacos...14

  Ratatouille 15

  Tomato Sauce 17

  Turkey Burgers 18

  Kombu & Konnyaku 19

  Sweet & Tangy Pasta...23

  Namasu...24

  Jerk Salmon...25

  Fish Tacos – 2nd recipe 27

  Cheesy Eggplant Pasta 28

  Easy-Peasy Egg Wraps 29

  Quick Grilled Vegetables...30

  Stir Fried Veggie Curry 31

  Vegan's Lasagne...32

  Saucy Parmesan Cheese Pasta...34

  Mashed Potato Platter 34

  Macaroni with Cheese..35

  Vermicelli Rice with Cinnamon 36

  Brussels Sprouts Galore...37

Cranberry Bliss 38

Cheese Casserole 38

Glazed Miso Chicken 39

Butter Melted Potatoes 39

Tarka 40

Sweet Potato Mix 41

Motley Rice 42

Mustard Cabbage Casserole 43

Chinese Mustard Greens 44

Zucchini 45

Steamed Fish & Scalllions with Peanut Oil 46

Desserts 47

Cinnamon Crusted Strawberry Flan 47

Cheese Spiced-up Pie 49

Cinnamon Carrot Pancakes 50

Veggie Pie 51

Cheddar Pie 52

Vanilla Apple Waffles 53

Sweet Potato Pie 54

Mango-Filled French Toast 57

Drinks 58

Cherry Chilled Milk Shake 58

Manana Smoothie 58

Cucumber Yogurt Shake 59

Salads 59

Vanilla Yogurt Tortellini 59

Tomato and Mac Salad 60

Olives & Egg Salad 60

Chicken Taco Salad 61

Cole Slaw Classic 62

Cranberry and Orange Salad 63

Dijon Mustard Vinaigrette 63

Cole Slaw 64

Eggplant Salad with Tomato Sauce 64

French Dressing Duex 65

Chunky Chicken Salad 66

Cranberry Jell-O Salad 67

Spicy-Chicken Caesar Salad 68

Fancy Pea Toss 69

Easy Honey Mustard 69

Ginger Salad Dressing 70

Hot Turnip and Dill Salad 71

Chili-Chinese Chicken Salad 72

Cauliflower Salad in Italian Dressing 73

Lime Vinaigrette 74

Waldorf Salad (Low Carb) 75

Munchy Mushroom Salad 76

Lemon Dressing 77

Spring Salad 78

Crunchy Sweet Chicken Salad 79

Tapenade 80

Yummy Curry-Glazed Cod Salad 81

Shades of Potato Salad 82

Sesame dressing 83

Watercress Salad 84

Crispy Kale Salad 85

Gai Choy Salad 86

Iceberg Salad 86

Mushroom Salad in Italian Dressing 87

Pecans and Pineapples Too! Salad 87

Snapper Salad 88

Spinach Salad 88

Side Salad 2 89

Sesame Seed Oriental Dressing 89

Simple Salad 90

Lettuce Mix Salad 91

Sweet Orange Marinade 92

Island Salad Dressing 92

Tuna & Goat Cheese Caesar Salad 93

Tuna Cheese Salad..93

Soups 94

Creamy Carrot and Turnip Soup 94

Chicken & Veal Soup...95

Perfect Pumpkin Soup 96

Onion and Milk Soup...97

Asparagus Soup...98

Ground Beef Soup 99

Codfish Treat Soup..100

Everything-in Vegetable soup...101

Chicken Soup for your Gout...102

Beans Beans Beans! Soup...103

Resources:...104

YumsUp.com 104

Traverse Bay Farms 104

Health Smart Recipes 105

Introduction,

Thank for purchasing the *No Gout Pain Cookbook* 3rd edition. I have added 15 new recipes in the 3rd edition.

Each recipe in this cookbook has been reviewed and approved by a nutritionist. This means you'll have the confidence to enjoy each recipe without the worry of an increased risk of a gout attack.

Best of all, these recipes are simple and taste great. You'll enjoy how each recipe is packed full of flavor without the worry of gout pain.

In addition, to following these low-purine, gout fighting recipes, you may want to also consider adding tart cherry juice to your daily routine. This is a powerful gout-fighting food.

Cherry juice is made from tart cherries. While I have included some recipes with cherries, drinking cherry juice daily will most certainly also help you to reduce to risk of a gout attack and it is a great way to stop future flair-ups.

Traverse Bay Farms, based in the cherry growing region of Northern Michigan, is the place I would recommend you check out for your 100% tart cherry juice.

Thank you and I hope you enjoy all of the great tasting recipes included in the *No Gout Pain Cookbook* 3rd edition,

Diane Sanders

Moist Chili Chicken

Serves: 4 Prep time: 10 minutes Cook time: 8 minutes

Ingredients

Dressing:

1/4 cup light ranch dressing
1/4 cup mild green salsa
2 tablespoons chopped fresh cilantro

Salad:

1 tablespoon chili powder
1/4 teaspoon ground cumin
1/4 teaspoon garlic powder
1/4 teaspoon onion powder
1/4 teaspoon salt
1/8 teaspoon ground black pepper
1 pound thin chicken breast slices or chicken tenders
1 lime quartered
6 cups shredded romaine lettuce
1 can (15 ounces) black beans, rinsed and drained
1/2 cup corn kernels
1 medium tomato, chopped
1/4 cup thinly sliced red onion

How To Do It

1. To make the dressing: In a small bowl, mix the ranch dressing, salsa, and cilantro until blended. Cover and refrigerate. To make the salad: Coat a barbecue grill or ridged grill pan with olive oil spray, and heat to medium-hot. In a cup, mix the chili powder, cumin, garlic powder, onion powder, salt, and pepper. Rub evenly on both sides of the chicken.
2. Grill the chicken, turning once, for 3 to 4 minutes, or until it is no longer pink and the juices run clear. Transfer to a plate. Squeeze the lime over the cooked chicken. In a large bowl, toss the romaine with half the dressing. Divide among 4 plates. Sprinkle the bean, corn, tomato, and red onion equally over each serving and top with the grilled chicken. Serve the remaining dressing on the side.

Saucy Spicy Chicken

Ingredients

Sauce

2 tbsp tomato paste
1/4 cup raw honey (better for gout diet)
1/4 cup low-sodium soy sauce
1/4 cup natural apple juice
1/4 cup broth or water

How To Do It

Combine ketchup, honey, soy sauce, juice/wine, and 1/4 cup broth/water and stir well to dissolve honey or sugar.

Ingredients
1 onion, sliced
3-6 cloves garlic, chopped
2 4-in. (20cm) slices of fresh ginger
1 stick of cinnamon, halved
3-4 pieces of whole star anise
6-10 whole black peppercorns
1 whole frying chicken
To Finish:
2 heaping tbsp of cornstarch
3 tbsp water

How To Do It
1. Stir together to dissolve cornstarch. Lay onion, garlic, ginger, cinnamon, star anise, and peppercorns on bottom of slow-cooker. Cut chicken into serving size pieces, and lay on top of spices. Add prepared Sauce, and enough additional broth/water to cover the chicken. Set slowcooker on LOW setting and leave to enjoy the rest of your morning.
2. 2. After 6-7 hours, remove chicken to serving dish and cover to keep warm. Strain remaining sauce into a skillet and boil over high heat to reduce to about 1.5 cups. Taste and if the flavor is not too concentrated, further reduce to 1 cup. If flavors are already strong, proceed to thickening.

3. Taste and correct seasoning. To thicken, reduce heat to medium and add cornstarch mixture, stirring well as you pour in cornstarch. Stir well to combine and cook until sauce is slightly thickened and takes on a shine. Pour over chicken.

Kajiki Ogo Combo

Ingredients

For the Fish:
2 4 oz. (120g) skinless fillets of firm-fleshed fish
1/2 tsp cumin powder
1/2 tsp coriander powder ground black pepper sea salt

Combine cumin and coriander powders, and gently massage or rub into fish. Set aside for at least 30 minutes. For the go: Take one large fist-full of raw ogo and place in colander. Rinse well. Bring 4 cups of water to a hard boil, and then pour over ogo in colander. Shake and drain well, then rinse with cold water and leave to dry while you prepare the dressing

For the Sauce and Dressing:

4 cloves garlic, minced olive oil
1/4 cup dry white wine
1/2 tsp coriander powder
1/2 tsp Aleppo pepper
1-1/2 tbsp pomegranate molasses
1-1/2 tbsp Manuka or other non-flowery honey
Sea salt, to taste
1 tbsp red wine or raspberry vinegar
1-2 tbsp olive oil sea salt, to taste

How To Do It

1. In a small saucepan set over low heat, sweat garlic in oil until softened, about 5-7 minutes. Add wine, and turn heat up to medium-high. Add coriander and pepper, and cook until spices are fragrant and alcohol has burned off, about 1 minute. Add molasses, honey and sea salt, and stir through. Cook together for about 1 minute.
2. Remove 2 tbsp of sauce to a small mixing bowl and whisk in vinegar and oil. Taste and correct for salt. Using kitchen shears, cut ogo into 2-inch pieces. Add to dressing and mix well. Set aside.
3. Heat skillet with 2 tbsp oil over high heat, salt fish fillets, then immediately add to pan, salted side down. When fillets release from pan, turn them over and reduce heat to medium. Cook until flesh will flake with a fork.

Lemons & Olives Chicken

Ingredients

1 3-4 lb. (1.5-2kg) chicken, cut into serving size
1 tsp cumin
1/2 tsp coriander
1/2 tsp sweet paprika
1/2 tsp freshly ground black pepper
1/4 cup dried tart cherries

Combine cumin, coriander, paprika and pepper. Rub spice mixture into chicken, especially under the skin and between the bone and breast meat, if using whole chicken. Set aside for at least 30 minutes, but as long as overnight in the fridge.
1 whole preserved lemon
Separate pulp and rinds. Cut rinds into thin slices, and place 3/4 of slices under the skin and between flesh of chicken, pre-heat oven to 350F/180C.

2 tbsp olive oil
1 medium onion, sliced thinly lengthwise
3 cloves garlic, coarsely chopped
3-4 bay leaves
1 - 1 and 1/2 cup whole olives, unpitted
1/2 cup (120ml) chicken broth
1/4 cup (60ml) dry white wine
2 tbsp juice from preserved lemons

How To Do It

1. Heat oil over medium-high in a large skillet. In batches, brown chicken and place in ovenproof casserole dish or Dutch oven. Turn heat down to medium-low, and In same oil cook onions until translucent, about 8-10 minutes. Add garlic and continue cooking together until garlic is fragrant.
2. Meanwhile, scatter remaining 1/4 of the lemon rinds and dried cherries over the casserole, and tuck bay leaves between chicken pieces. Add lemon pulp (optional step) and olives to the dish, and evenly distribute the onions and garlic over the chicken. Add broth, wine and lemon juice. Cover and bake in pre-heated oven for 45 minutes. Scatter remaining dried cherries over the casserole. Serve with couscous and a crisp green or tomato salad.

Eggplant Circles

Serves: 4 Prep time: 15 minutes Cook time: 25 minutes

Ingredients

1 15 oz can organic crushed tomatoes with basil
1/2 can (7 oz) artichoke hearts
1 large grilled eggplant
2 cherry peppers
2 jalapenos
5-6 garlic cloves
1 large organic carrot
2-3 sun dried tomatoes (sulphur free) handful chopped fresh Portobello mushrooms
nutritional yeast, to taste splash dry red wine, optional

Spices Rosemary, Oregano, Garlic powder Crushed red pepper, Sea salt, Pepper, dash of
Italian seasoning

How To Do It

1. Slice the eggplant width wise into ~1/8 to 1/4" slices for round eggplant pieces.
   Season with your choice of spices and spray the grill. I seasoned the eggplant with a
   blend of turmeric, ground black peppercorns, a dash of cayenne pepper, oregano,
   rosemary, garlic powder, a bit of dried crushed red pepper, thyme, and sea salt .
   Add the eggplant and whole peppers to the grill. Close the grill and cook on high for
   about 10-15 minutes or until very tender.
2. Meanwhile, chop your mushrooms and sun-dried tomatoes, and shred the carrot. If
   you're using dehydrated mushrooms, steep them in boiling water high enough to
   cover them, and leave them covered for about 10 minutes or until soft. Drain the
   mushrooms. Set the chopped and shredded ingredients aside.
3. Add about half of the chopped sundried tomatoes and red wine to the tomato sauce
   and stir. Spray the bottom of an oven-safe glass baking dish with non-stick spray.
   Use a small Pyrex and spread the sauce lightly, covering the bottom. Layer the
   grilled eggplant slices on the bottom of the dish, from large to small slices. Cover the
   yeast and eggplant with a thin layer of the prepared carrots, jalapenos, mushrooms,
   and sundried tomatoes. Cover that layer with sauce, then add another layer, sauce,
   and repeat.
4. Top the casserole with a layer of sauce and the artichoke hearts. If using canned
   artichokes, drain thoroughly and layer directly on top of the casserole. If you're
   using fresh artichoke, steam or grill them, then, once cooled, cut them into small
   pieces and add to the top. Bake at 450 degrees for about 25 minutes. Note that the
   short time is for the convection oven setting I used. If you aren't using convection,
   baking may take longer. Serve hot.

Fish Tacos

Serves: 4 Prep time: 15 minutes Cook time: 35 minutes

Ingredients

2 1lb. fillets of skinned white-meat fish, such as ahi or snapper Juice of 1 large lemon, about 3 TBL.
1 tsp cumin
1 tbsp oil
Combine lemon juice, cumin and oil. Place fish in glass or other non-reactive dish, pour marinade over fillets and coat all sides. Cover and refrigerate at least 30 minutes.

Garlic Sauce 2 cloves garlic, peeled and chopped
1/2 tsp. salt
1 cup mayonnaise
3-4 tbsp milk (optional)

How To Do It

1. Place garlic and salt in mortar and grind to make a smooth paste. Combine with mayo and milk, if using, to reach desired consistency. Set aside to serve. To assemble: 1 medium head of cabbage, finely shredded 2 limes, quartered 20-30 fresh corn tortillas, warmed and kept covered sliced pickled jalapenos (not traditional) homemade or bottled salsa (not traditional)
2. Remove fish from marinade and lightly pat dry. Season with sea salt and ground black pepper. Grill or broil for 5 minutes on each side, or until fish flakes easily with a fork.

Immediately dress with fresh squeezed lime juice, and flake meat with fork. Place warmed tortillas, cabbage, garlic sauce and other optional garnishes at the table with flaked fish. Let each person make their own tacos as they eat. Can be served with rice and beans, too.

Ratatouille

Serves: 2 Prep time: 15 minutes Cook Time: 40 minutes

Ingredients

Olive oil
1 1/2 lbs. long Japanese eggplant, halved lengthwise and sliced
1 1/2 lbs. small or medium zucchini, halved lengthwise and sliced
1 large yellow onion, diced
4 cloves garlic, finely diced
1 medium green bell pepper, seeded and diced
1/2 tsp ground coriander
1 tsp white pepper
1 1/2 lbs. Roma tomatoes, peeled, seeded and diced
1/4 cup julienned fresh basil
2 tbsp minced fresh Italian parsley
sea salt to taste

How To Do It

1. Preheat large sauté pan on medium heat. Add enough oil to coat bottom of pan, and add eggplant to cover pan (may have to do in batches). Lightly brown both sides and remove from heat. Add more oil and repeat with rest of eggplant. Repeat process with zucchini. Lower heat and in the same pan cook onion until translucent (this may take 8-10 minutes). Add garlic and bell pepper after first 5 minutes. When onions are translucent, add coriander and white pepper and cook another 1 minute.
2. Raise heat to medium-high and add tomatoes, basil and parsley, and cook uncovered 10 minutes. Taste sauce and season with salt. Add back eggplant and zucchini, cover and simmer 15- 20 minutes or until vegetables are tender, but not falling apart. A crispy, light baguette (on Oahu, St. Germain's demi-baguettes are the closest to the real thing we've found) and a nice pinot noir or syrah (depending on your tolerance for tannin) will round out your meal.
3. While we would absolutely love to pair this with a wine from France's Bourgogne or Rhone regions, we try to drink as close to home as possible. Since Hawaii doesn't (yet) have a robust home-grown viticulture, we look to West Coast and Australian wines to fill the bill for now.

Beans & Cherries Chicken

Ingredients

Chicken Meatballs
1 lb. (450g) ground chicken
1/2 medium onion, minced
1 clove garlic
1 large egg
1 tsp paprika
2 tsp oregano
1 tsp cumin
1/2 tsp Aleppo pepper (optional)
1 tsp sea salt
1 tsp ground black pepper

How To Do It

1. Combine all ingredients and shape into golf-ball sized rounds. Sauté in pan lined with 1/2-inch oil until browned on all sides, or place on baking sheet, drizzle with olive oil, and bake in tabletop oven for 20 minutes. Add hot to sauce, or cool completely and freeze to make ahead (add to sauce frozen after beans have simmered for 20 minutes, then cook for another 40 minutes).
2. To use fresh chicken, use 1 lb. skinless, boneless chicken breast or thigh meat cut into 1-inch cubes. Combine paprika, cumin, peppers and salt (omit oregano) listed in Meatball recipe above, and coat diced chicken in dry mixture. Set aside 30 minutes, then add to Tomato Sauce below after beans have simmered for 20 minutes, then continue cooking for the remaining 40 minutes in the original recipe.

Tomato Sauce

4 tbsp olive oil
1 medium onion, diced
2 cloves garlic, minced
1/4 cup dried cherries (or currants, raisins, sultanas)
1 tbsp dried oregano
1/2 tsp dried thyme
1 tsp dried dill (optional)
6 ripe tomatoes, or 1 28oz. (780g) canned tomatoes, diced
1/2 cup dry white wine, or chicken or vegetable broth
1/2 bunch fresh Italian parsley (flat-leaf), about 1 cup chopped
1 bay leaf
1 lb. green beans

How To Do It

1. In large sauté pan set over low heat, sweat onions in olive oil until transparent (take your time; this will take 8-10 minutes at least). Add garlic and dried cherries, and cook until both are just softened. Add oregano, thyme and dill (if using), and mix through onion mixture and leave to cook about 2 minutes, or until herbs become fragrant.
2. Turn heat up to medium high and immediately add tomatoes, wine/broth, parsley and bay leaf. (If you omit the dried fruit completely, add 1/2 tsp. brown sugar to sauce.) Partially cover, and leave to simmer 20 minutes while you prepare beans.
3. Wash and tip green beans to remove stringy spine. Leave whole or cut into 2-inch lengths, it's up to your own aesthetics and who you are cooking for. Add to tomato sauce, cover completely and let simmer over low heat for 30-40 minutes. Add cooked meatballs, cover and simmer another 30 minutes.

Turkey Burgers

Serves: 4 Prep time: 5 minutes Cook time: 16 minutes

Ingredients

1 pound lean ground turkey breast
2 cups sliced mushrooms
1/4 cup chopped fresh parsley
1-1/2 tablespoons Worcestershire sauce
1/2 teaspoon onion salt
1 tablespoon vegetable oil
4 hamburger buns split

How To Do It

1. In a large bowl, combine the turkey, 1 cup of the mushrooms, the parsley, Worcestershire sauce, and onion salt. With clean hands, mix the ingredients until thoroughly combined and shape into equal-size patties. Set aside. Warm the oil in a large skillet over medium heat. When hot, add the remaining 1 cup of mushrooms and cook, stirring, for 2 minutes, or until brown. Transfer the mushrooms to a plate and cover to keep warm.
2. Place the patties in the skillet over medium heat and cook, turning occasionally, for 12 to 14 minutes, or until a thermometer inserted in the center registers 165°F and the meat is no longer pink. Set the patties on the buns, top with the sautéed mushrooms, and serve.

Kombu & Konnyaku

Ingredients

1 packet dashi no moto
2 tsp mirin
1 tsp sugar, light brown
Prepare the pork and broth, 1.5-2lb whole pork belly
or shoulder. 1 small hand ginger, washed well and sliced in ½ inch slices, 3 tbsp
whisky, sake, or awamori (Okinawan sake)

Broth preparation

Wash pork well and place in large (8qt or larger) pot with ginger. Cover meat with
water and bring to boil. Reduce heat to medium and skim foam off top. Add liquor, then
cover with lid and let simmer for 45 minutes. Remove meat and set aside. Discard
ginger. Add dashi no moto, mirin and sugar to broth and keep at simmer.

2 strands of Hayani kombu, soaked in 6 qts water or at least 20 minutes
1 piece Konnyaku
1 small white radish, peeled and cut in 3 in. pieces
2 large carrots, peeled and cut on diagonal
4-6 pieces fresh or canned whole bamboo tips, cut into 3-in pieces
8 pieces dried shiitake mushroom, soaked in 4 cups water until completely rehydrated;
about 1 hour
1 stick chikuwa kamaboko
1 large firm block of tofu, wrapped in towel and drained in fridge at least 1 hr.,then cut
in 2-in. Cubes
2-3 tsp Kikkoman soy sauce

Note: save soaking water and strain. Fresh shiitake may be used, but dried is preferred
for its intense flavor

Kombu Preparation

Depending on type of kombu, may need longer soak – it should be pliable but not
disintegrating. Remove kombu and save water, if you like. If rehydrated kombu is more
than 6" across, cut lengthwise before proceeding. Start tying knots in kombu strand,
leaving about 4" between each knot. Now cut evenly between knots.

Konnyaku preparation

1. Rinse well. Slice cross-wise into ½" slices—about 12 slices. Cut a lengthwise slit in the center of each slice, leaving ¾" uncut at top and bottom—you should be able to put a finger through the hole. Now the fun part—hold one slice in your left hand, and with your right, push the bottom of the slice through the slit and out. It will create a very attractive spiral pattern in the center. After you're done admiring your handiwork, add to broth.
2. Add Kombu, 1 cup saved Kombu water, konnyaku, shiitake and shiitake water to broth. Simmer about 30 minutes. Add carrots, daikon, bamboo, kamaboko and tofu. Slice pork into 2" pieces and add to broth with soy sauce. Simmer another 20 minutes or until Kombu is tender at the knotted middle (test the thickest part with fork -- it should slide easily through). Serve with rice, and Japanese hot mustard or wasabi, and soy sauce for dipping. Pickled vegetables, called tsukemono, are also lovely with this. Enjoy!

Grilled Chicken (Persian)

Ingredients

Marinade

1/4 cup (30g) plain full-fat yogurt
1/2 cup olive oil
4-6 cloves garlic, minced
Juice from 1 lemon (about 1/4 cup, 60ml)
2 tsp cumin powder
1/2 tsp saffron threads, soaked in 2 tbsp water Sea salt Ground black pepper
1 whole chicken, backbone removed,
Quartered, and wing tips removed
1 lime, quartered

Directions

Combine marinade ingredients in glass bowl or zipper bag. Add chicken, and combine well, massaging marinade under skin and into joints. Cover or zip up, and let marinate at least 8 hours, and up to 3 days.

To prepare to grill, remove chicken from refrigerator about 30 minutes before it is set to go on the grill (i.e., while the grill is pre-heating or the charcoal coming up to cooking temperature). Make basting sauce.

Basting Sauce:

Juice of 1 lime (about 2 tsp.)
3 tbsp unsalted butter, melted sea salt ground black pepper

How To Do It

1. Combine ingredients and blend well to dissolve salt. Remove chicken from marinade and discard marinade. Place chicken on grill, skin-side down first; turn over and baste liberally. Grill until each piece runs clear when cut near the joint, basting each time the chicken is turned. Remove fully cooked chicken from grill, and immediately squeeze lime juice over.
2. Serve with lavish, basmati rice, grilled vegetables, yogurt salad, and liberally sprinkled with sumac. Note on cutting chicken for serving: In the U.S., we

generally cut a half-breast at the joint between breast and wing, leaving a tasty but tiny wing piece and a rather oversized breast portion. Here's a more equitable cut—cut through the lower third of the breast so some white meat goes with the wing, and further divide the remaining part in two. This will allow more diners to get a share of white meat, if they like, and it encourages portion control as well.

Sweet & Tangy Pasta

Serves: 2

Wash and rinse stalks and greens. Cut along both sides of each stalk to separate the greens. Roll the greens lengthwise and cut along the width into 1-inch pieces. Either slice the stalks in thin slices on the diagonal, or cut into 4-inch lengths, then de-vein each length (similar to cleaning celery fibres). Slice each length into 5-6 long pieces.

Ingredients

3-4 cloves garlic, sliced
2 tbsp + 1 tbsp olive oil
3 oz. (85g) lean pork,cut into slivers 1-inch long (optional)
1/2 tsp sea salt
1/4 cup (40g) currants
1 tsp raw sugar
1/3 cup (80ml) red wine vinegar
12 oz. dried pasta

How To Do It

1. Start water for pasta. Heat first 2 tbsp oil in large skillet (large enough to hold pasta too) over medium heat, Add garlic, and cook until fragrant and lightly browned. Add pork, if using, and cook until browned, about 4-5 minutes. Add beet stalks and salt, and stir well to coat with oil.
2. Cover pan and allow to cook until stalks begin to wilt, about 3 minutes. Increase that to medium-high, and add beet greens and 1 tbsp oil, cover and cook for 5 minutes. Remove cover and sprinkle sugar and currants over greens, stir through. Make a hole in the center of the greens, and pour vinegar in hole.
3. Stir everything through, and allow to cook for another 8-10 minutes or until greens are bright green and softened. Taste and correct seasoning, and keep sauce warm until pasta is cooked. Salt water and add pasta — cook to al dente. Drain well but do not rinse. Add pasta to sauce. Increase heat under skillet to medium-high, and stir through to combine pasta and sauce ingredients. Serve in warmed bowls/plates, garnish with squeeze of lemon, if desired.

Namasu

Ingredients

1 lb. (450g) daikon, scrubbed, peeled
1 small carrot (100-120g), scrubbed and peeled
2 tsp sugar
1 tsp salt
2 tbsp dried wakame seaweed, placed in a bowl and covered with 4 cups cool water for 20-30 minutes (not longer)

How To Do It

1. Slice daikon lengthwise, then into thin half-moon slices. Place in colander and sprinkle with sugar, then mix well and leave 30-40 minutes to drain. Sugar will pull water from the radish and leave it pliable but crunchy. Do not rinse.
2. Using your peeler, slice thin ribbons of carrot from the root. Cut the ribbons into fourths across their width. Place in colander, sprinkle with salt and leave for 20-40 minutes to drain. Do not rinse. Place wakame in small bowl and cover with 3 cups cool water for 20-30 minutes. Rinse in 2-3 changes of water. Squeeze dry. Combine daikon, carrot, and wakame in medium bowl.

Dressing

1/2 packet dashi-no-moto (dried bonito broth)
1/3 cup warm water
1 tsp. sugar
1/3 cup rice vinegar or white wine vinegar
1 tbsp mirin
1 tbsp fresh lemon juice

Combine dressing ingredients in small bowl in the order listed above. Whisk or stir well to dissolve sugar and dashi-no-moto. Taste and correct seasoning — it should taste lemony and ever so-slightly sweet. Pour over vegetables and leave in refrigerator at least 30 minutes. Keep in refrigerator up to 5 days.

Jerk Salmon

Serves: 4

Ingredients

For the fish: Pat fillets dry. Sprinkle with lime juice, and then coat both sides of fish with jerk rub. Allow to marinate while you start the stew. 4 4-6oz. (113 - 170g) fillets of Alaskan sockeye salmon (or halibut, or snapper) Purchased jerk seasoning powdered rub Juice of 1 lime sea salt

For the stew:

1 bag frozen cut okra
1 bag frozen sweet corn
1 15oz (425g) can diced tomatoes
1/2 tsp dried oregano
1/2 cup (120ml) water or broth sea salt, to taste ground black pepper, to taste

How To Do It

1. Combine all ingredients in a skillet (large enough to hold all the fish fillets too). Bring stew to a boil, then cover and reduce heat to a simmer. Allow to simmer for 45 minutes to 1 hour, depending on how well you like your okra done.
2. After the stew has simmered for 30 minutes and pre-heat a second skillet for the fish. Season fish fillets with salt to taste (remember the stew has salt too). Add oil, then fish to the pan and allow the seasonings to brown (it will look like Cajun blackened fish), about 2 minutes. Brown the other side of the fillets (they will not be cooked through).
3. Check stew and correct seasoning, adding a little water or broth if it looks dry. Add fish on top, just below the surface of the stew. Cover and cook for the last 10 minutes. Serve with biscuits or garlic bread.

Classic Monchong Bake

For the Humus:
1 cup of dried chickpeas, soaked in water to cover at least 8 hours

Ingredients

Drain chickpeas, place in 4-quart or larger saucepan, and cover with by the least 2" of clean water.
Bring to a boil, then lower heat to a simmer and cook for 1 hour. Add 1/2 tsp of sea salt, and cook for another 30 minutes or until beans are easily pierced with a toothpick but not mushy (cooking time will depend on the hardness of your water). Turn off heat, cover and let cool in pan.
2 tbsp liquid reserved from cooking chickpeas
1/2 tsp sea salt
2-4 cloves garlic, minced
5 tbsp lemon juice
4 tbsp olive oil
1/3 cup tahini

How To Do It

1. Place ingredients in the order listed above into food processor or blender. Last, add drained cooked chickpeas or 2 15 oz. canned low-salt chickpeas. If you prefer your humus with a little texture, reserve a 1/4 cup of chickpeas. Puree the mix until smooth. If using a blender and the mixture is too thick, taste a little and see if it needs more lemon juice or water, and add accordingly. If you've reserved some chickpeas, add them in and pulse briefly to break them up a bit. Taste again and correct for salt, lemon juice or olive oil. Set aside for at least an hour if using as a dip. For the Fish: 2 6 oz. filets of monchong, cleaned and patted dry, sea salt and ground black pepper2. To coat fish, season fish fillet with sea salt and ground black pepper. Layer a generous amount of hummous to one side of the fish. Measure the thickness of the fillets at the thickest point. Set aside for at least 30 minutes while oven and pan pre-heat. Pre-heat oven and oven-proof skillet or baking dish to 450F/230C. Add 2 tbsp olive oil to heated skillet or baking dish, and place fillets, hummous-side up, on the skillet or dish. 3. Place in pre-heated oven and bake for 10 minutes for every 1" of fish. If top crust has not sufficiently browned by the time fish is cooked, set oven to broil for a minute to brown the humus crust. Garnish with a pinch of paprika or chili (red pepper) powder, if desired.

Serve with your choice of starch and vegetable.

Fish Tacos – 2nd recipe

Serves: 4

2 1lb. fillets of skinned white-meat fish
Juice of 1 large lemon, about 3 tbsp
1 tsp cumin
1 tbsp oil
Combine lemon juice, cumin and oil. Place fish in glass or other non-reactive dish, pour marinade over fillets and coat all sides. Cover and refrigerate at least 30 minutes.

Garlic Sauce

2 cloves garlic, peeled and chopped
1/2 tsp salt
1 cup mayonnaise
3-4 tbsp milk (optional)

How To Do It

1. Place garlic and salt in mortar and grind to make a smooth paste. Combine with mayo and milk, if using, to reach desired consistency. Set aside to serve. To assemble: 1 medium head of cabbage finely shredded. 2 limes, quartered 20-30 fresh corn tortillas, warmed and kept covered. sliced pickled jalapenos (not traditional)homemade or bottled salsa (not traditional)
2. Remove fish from marinade and lightly pat dry, season with sea salt and ground black pepper. Grill or broil for 5 minutes on each side, or until fish flakes easily with a fork. Immediately dress with fresh squeezed lime juice, and flake meat with fork. Place warmed tortillas, cabbage, garlic sauce and other optional garnishes at the table with flaked fish. Let each person make their own tacos as they eat. Can be served with rice and beans, too.

Cheesy Eggplant Pasta

Serves: 2 Prep time: 10 minutes Cook time: 12 minutes

Ingredients

8 ounces penne
1/4 cup sun-dried tomatoes
1/4 cup diced eggplant
1/4 cup diced zucchini
2 tablespoons olive oil
2 tablespoons Parmesan cheese
1/2 cup mozzarella cubes
5 leaves fresh basil, chopped
Sea salt and freshly ground pepper to taste

How To Do It

Boil pasta for five minutes or according to package directions. Drain. Sauté vegetables in one tablespoon olive oil for four minutes. Remove from heat. In a frying pan, cook the pasta and vegetables in one tablespoon olive oil for three minutes and remove from heat. Mix in the Parmesan and mozzarella cheeses and basil leaves. Season with freshly ground black pepper, sea salt, and more olive oil to taste.

Easy-Peasy Egg Wraps

Serves: 2 Prep time: 5 minutes Cook time: 9 minutes

Ingredients:

1/3 cup chopped sweet white onion or scallion
1/4 cup chopped red bell pepper
1 cup egg substitute
Salt
Ground black pepper
1/3 cup shredded reduced-fat cheese of your choice
2 whole wheat soft taco wraps (8" in diameter)
1/4 cup salsa

How To Do It

1. Coat a medium non-stick skillet with cooking spray and heat over medium heat. Add the onion or scallion and bell pepper. Cook, stirring often, 5 minutes, or until tender. pour in the egg substitute, and season to taste with salt and pepper. Cook, stirring often, until the eggs are almost set.
2. Remove the skillet from the heat and sprinkle with the cheese. Cover and let stand for 1 minute, or until the cheese has melted. Spoon the egg mixture onto the warmed wraps, and top with the salsa. Roll up the wraps, folding in the sides.

Quick Grilled Vegetables

Serves: 4 Prep time: 10 minutes Cook time: 15 minutes

Ingredients

1 tbsp Extra Virgin Olive Oil
2 tbsp Balsamic Vinegar
1 tsp Oregano, ground
1 cup Butternut Squash, sliced
1 cup Zucchini, sliced
1 cup Green Pepper, Raw, sliced
1 cup Red Pepper, Raw, sliced

How To Do It

Slice vegetables in long pieces, suitable for grilling on the barbecue. Place on perforated grilling sheet and cook on barbecue on medium heat. Mix the oil, vinegar and oregano and use for basting the vegetables while they cook. The liquid should be sufficient to continue basting the length of time that the veggies cook. This is a huge family favourite in the hot summer months.

Stir Fried Veggie Curry

Serves: 2 Prep time: 10 minutes Cook time: 10 minutes

Ingredients

2 tbsp oyster sauce
1 tbsp soy sauce
1/2 tsp chili powder
1/2 tbsp peanut oil
7 oz. tofu, drained and diced
1 med red bell pepper, diced
1 med yellow bell pepper, diced
1 cup mushrooms, slices
1 1/2 cup Pak-choi, whites diced, greens shredded
1 cup vegetable broth
2 tsp curry powder
1 tbsp cornstarch
2 cups brown rice, cooked

How To Do It

In a small bowl, combine first 4 ingredients. Pour over tofu cubes and allow marinating for at least an hour. Put tofu, pak-choi and mushrooms in a large pan or wok and stir-fry for a few minutes. Add both peppers and stir-fry for five more minutes, until everything is tender crisp. Combine vegetable broth, curry powder and cornstarch, and add to wok. Simmer until the sauce has become thick. Serve the veggie sauce on top of the brown rice.

Vegan's Lasagne

Serves: 8

Prep time: 15 minutes
Cook time: 1 hour 15 minutes

Ingredients

Sauce
1 tbsp olive oil
2 cloves minced garlic
2 medium chopped onions
1 red pepper chopped
10 oz. sliced mushrooms
4 tsp oregano
1 1/2 tsp basil
1 1/2 tbsp soy sauce
1 small can tomato paste
1 16oz can tomato sauce
1/2 cup red wine

Lasagne
1 package (thawed) chopped spinach - squeeze out water
1/2 tsp nutmeg
2 cups low fat cottage cheese
1/3 cup grated romano
1 egg
1 egg white
8oz lasagne noodles
1 ½ cup skim shredded mozzarella

How To Do It

1. Sauce: Stir fry garlic, onions, red pepper, mushrooms, oregano & basil in olive oil. Cook until all liquid evaporates (~15 min). Add soy sauce, tomato paste, tomato sauce, & red wine. Boil & use while hot. Lasagne: Cook lasagne noodles. Mix spinach (or broccoli), nutmeg, cottage cheese, romano, egg & egg white.

2. Spread 1/4 of tomato sauce in bottom of 9x13 pan. Put 1 layer of noodles over sauce. Spread 1/3 spinach mix over noodles, then tomato sauce. Continue to layer, end with tomato sauce. Spread mozzarella over top. Cover tightly with aluminium foil. Bake 1 hour at 375.

Saucy Parmesan Cheese Pasta

Serves: 4
Prep time: 5 minutes
Cook time: 9 minutes

Ingredients

1 lb pasta (thin noodles)
4 tbsp chopped coriander
1c parmesan cheese (grated)
6 tbsp olive oil
2 cloves of garlic (crushed or finely chopped)
tsp pepper
tsp salt

How To Do It

Boil the noodles according to the directions on the package. After draining the pasta put it into a serving bowl. Mix all of the remaining ingredients and thoroughly combine. Serve this meal while still hot and enjoy.

Mashed Potato Platter

Serves: 2

Ingredients

4 radishes (medium)
2 c mashed potatoes
8 black olives (sliced thin and pitted)
8 cloves garlic (crushed)
c plain yogurt (low fat)
6 tbsp olive oil
1 tsp black pepper
1 tsp salt

How To Do It
Combine garlic, potatoes, salt, yogurt, olive oil, pepper, and salt. Put mixture on a platter and decorate with radishes and olives. Serve chilled.

Macaroni with Cheese

Serves: 4
Prep time: 15 minutes
Cook time: 50 minutes

Ingredients

4 tbsp butter
1 large onion, finely chopped
4 cups cooked macaroni
1 tsp salt
½ tsp pepper
1½ cups milk
¼ pound thinly sliced cheddar cheese

How To Do It

Melt butter in a frying pan, then sauté onion over medium heat for 12 minutes. Stir in remaining ingredients, except cheese, and then transfer frying pan contents to a greased casserole. Top evenly with cheese and bake uncovered in a 350° F preheated oven for 40 minutes. Serve from the casserole while warm.

Vermicelli Rice with Cinnamon

Serves: 4
Prep time: 10 minutes
Cook time: 45 minutes

Ingredients

4 Tbsp. butter
½ cup thin vermicelli, broken into small pieces
1 cup rice, rinsed
2¼ cups boiling water
¾ tsp. salt
¼ tsp. pepper
¼ tsp. cinnamon

How To Do It

1. In a frying pan, melt butter then sauté vermicelli over medium/low heat, stirring often, until the pieces just begin to turn golden brown. Add rice; stir-fry for further 1 minute. Stir in remaining ingredients, except cinnamon, and then bring to boil.
2. Cover and cook over low heat for 12 minutes. Turn off heat; stir. Re-cover and allow to cook in own steam for 30 minutes. Place on a platter, lightly sprinkle with cinnamon and serve as a side dish with vegetable stew entrees.

Brussels Sprouts Galore

Ingredients

1.25 lbs. (1/2 kilo) brussel sprouts, trimmed
2 tbsp unsalted butter
1 tbsp black mustard seeds
1/2 tsp ground coriander seed
2 tsp cumin
1 tsp turmeric
1 tsp salt
3-5 tbsp dried unsweetened coconut
3 tbsp coconut milk
salt

How To Do It

1. Boil water and briefly blanch sprouts (no more than a couple of minutes). Drain (keep some of the water) and cool. (I skipped this step) Heat butter in pan and add mustard seeds. When seeds begin to pop (I love the smell of popping mustard seeds! It's like spicy popcorn), add ground coriander, cumin, turmeric, salt and coconut. Warm spices.
2. If using coconut milk, add now. Add sprouts and coat with spices. Cover and lower heat. If not using coconut milk, add sprouts and coat with spice mixture. Keep the mixture moving in pan so spices don't burn. You may want to add some water from the blanching if the pan is too dry. Cook until sprouts are just tender and still bright green. Remove from heat immediately.

Cranberry Bliss

Serves: 6 Prep time: 5 minutes Cook time: 15 minutes

Ingredients

1 cup dark rum
1 teaspoon lemon rind, grated
3/4 cup artificial sweetener (or use sugar)
3/4 to 1 cup 1/2 cup walnuts, chopped, pecans or almonds
4 cups cranberries –raw fresh or frozen

How To Do It

Put Splenda and rum in saucepan, heat to boiling. Add cranberries& lemon zest, bring back to boil & immediately lower heat so the mixture is on a low, rolling boil, just above a simmer. Cover and cook for 10 minutes, stirring occasionally. Add chopped nuts, mixing in thoroughly Let cook 1-2 min, then remove from heat, cover and let cool completely. The rum & lemon zest add tremendous richness complexity to the sauce. But, if you want to forego the rum, just substitute an equal amount of water.

Cheese Casserole

Serves: 8 Prep time: 10 minutes Cook time: 45-50 minutes

Ingredients

3 eggs, slightly beaten
3 cups cottage cheese
Small diced onion black pepper to taste

How To Do It

Mix all ingredients and pour into a casserole dish. Bake at 350 degrees for 45-50 minutes, or until firm and pulls away from the sides of the pan. Serve warm.

Glazed Miso Chicken

Ingredients

1lb (450g) boneless chicken
3/4 cup (375ml) water
1/2 cup sake, or dry sherry, or apple juice
1 slice fresh ginger
2 tbsp mirin
3 tbsp sugar
4 tbsp white miso paste

How To Do It

Combine water, sake and ginger in sauté pan. Lay chicken in pan, and bring liquid to a boil, then reduce heat to simmer and cook about 5 minutes. Turn chicken over in pan, and add mirin, sugar and miso paste. Cover and simmer another 5 minutes. Remove cover and continue cooking until liquid thickens and coats chicken. Turn meat to glaze both sides. Remove from heat. Garnish with green onions, or sesame seeds.

Butter Melted Potatoes

Ingredients

2 large baking potatoes (about 1lb/.5kg)
3 tbsp unsalted butter
2 tbsp Bhel chutney, or date chutney
1 tsp honey
2 tsp chaat masala
1 tsp cayenne powder

How To Do It

Peel and cut potatoes into 1 inch dice. Melt butter in pan and fry potatoes on all sides. Mix together chutney and honey in large bowl. Combine chaat masala and cayenne powder. Remove cooked potato cubes into bowl with chutney/honey mix, and coat well. Immediately sprinkle masala/chilli mix and mix to coat well. Let cool a bit so flavors will blend.

Tarka

Ingredients

2/3 cup (160g) lentils, split peas or mung beans
2 cups (500ml) water
1 tsp turmeric
1 tsp cumin
1 tsp salt
For the Tarka
3-4 tbsp unsalted butter
1 medium onion, diced
3-4 cloves garlic
1-3 dried red chillies (had to leave these out this time)

How To Do It

Boil together the pulses, water, spices and salt. When the water reaches a boil, lower heat and simmer about 20 minutes or until the pulse reaches a soft consistency. Meanwhile, prepare the tarka. Sauté onions and garlic in butter until onions are translucent and starting to brown. Add crushed chillies and warm through. Remove from heat. Add half of tarka to cooked dal and stir well. Remove dal to serving bowl and garnish top with remaining tarka.

Sweet Potato Mix

Ingredients

2 lbs. of sweet potatoes
2 tbsp olive oil
1 tbsp brown mustard seeds
1 medium red onion, diced
1 jalapeno pepper, seeded and diced
2 tsp cumin powder
1 medium red cabbage (about 2 lbs/1kg), sliced lengthwise into 1-inch (2.5cm) wide slices
sea salt
1 tsp chaat masala
cilantro for garnish

How To Do It

1. Heat oil over medium high heat in large sauté pan or wok. When hot, add mustard seeds and stir until they begin popping, then immediately add onion. Stir to coat onion, then cover pan and turn heat to low. Allow onions to cook until translucent, about 8-10 minutes. Remove cover and return heat to medium high.
2. Move onions aside, creating a space in the middle of the pan, and add cumin powder to the center, stirring well to cook through for 1 minute. Add peppers, and sauté for another 5 minutes. Add cabbage and 1 tsp sea salt, mix well. Cover and cook until cabbage is tender, about 15 minutes.
3. Stir in prepared Mashed Sweet Potatoes and mix well to combine. Cover and heat through completely. Sprinkle with chaat masala and garnish with minced cilantro. Serve with any grilled fish or meat. Or eat either rolled in or atop (like a pizza) your favorite homemade or purchased flatbread. You can also shape into patties and pan fry with olive oil — the stickier texture of the sweet potato means no egg is required for binding — for entree-type cutlets.

Motley Rice

Ingredients

150g (3/4 cup) regular brown rice
150g (1/2 cup) white medium grain rice

How To Do It

1. Rinse brown rice well, and drain. Cover rice with water to 1-inch (4cm) over the top of the rice. Allow to soak for at least 8 hours. (Do this in the morning before you go to work.) When ready to cook, rinse white rice well, and drain. Repeat, until rinse water runs clear. Drain brown rice. Combine white and brown rice together, and add to rice cooker. Add 1-1/4 cup (320ml) water. Turn on rice cooker and allow to cook/steam. After rice cooker turns itself off, allow rice to finish steaming and do not open lid for at least 15 minutes, but no longer than 30.
2. Open lid, and with a clean towel, wipe condensation from sides and lid of rice cooker. With a rice paddle or spatula, gently turn rice over, bringing the rice on the bottom to the top in a folding motion (as you would fold in egg whites to a cake batter). Rice is ready to serve. Leftover mestizo rice makes great fried rice, especially with pineapple and spices. Read more about making Fried Rice.

Mustard Cabbage Casserole

Ingredients

1 large bunch mustard cabbage, stemmed and diced/julienned
2-3 tbsp olive oil
4-6 cloves garlic, chopped
1/4 cup chicken or vegetable broth, or water
1/2 tsp sea salt (optional)
1/2 tsp ground black pepper (optional)

How To Do It

1. Heat oil in wok over medium-high heat. Add garlic and stir to release fragrance and gently brown, then remove garlic and keep aside. Add cleaned mustard greens stem pieces to oil, add broth, cover and let cook 10-20 minutes, or until beginning to soften.
2. Stir to mix well, then add leafy parts of cabbage, cover and cook another 5-8 minutes, or until leafy parts are bright green. Remove cover and allow broth to reduce by half. Season to taste with sea salt and pepper, if using. Remove to serving plate and garnish with browned garlic.
3. We serve this as a side dish with any meal, from meatloaf and mashed potatoes, to rice and pan-seared tofu (Okinawan Champuru). I especially enjoy gai choy prepared this way and served with its garlicky pan gravy on top of mashed potatoes for a filling and delicious non-meat meal.

Chinese Mustard Greens

Serves: 4 as a side dish, 2 as an entrée Prep time: 15 minutes Cook time: 45 minutes

Ingredients

2 medium potatoes scrubbed and peeled
Slice potatoes cross-wise into thin slices. Toss with olive oil to prevent browning. Then sprinkle with sea salt and ground black or white pepper, Pre-heat oven to 350F/180C.
Olive oil
1 large head of Chinese mustard greens, washed well
4-6 cloves of garlic, sliced
1 cup chicken or vegetable broth
Sea salt, to taste
Ground black pepper, or white pepper

How To Do It

1. After washing greens well, separate thick stems from leaves. Slice stems in julienne. Cut leaves lengthwise, then finely shred — you should have 8-10 cups of leaves. Place stems, then leaves in large (10-12 cup) oven-safe casserole.
2. Add garlic, broth, 2 tbsp of olive oil and seasoning to taste. Layer potatoes over greens in overlapping rings. You may have to press to fit the potatoes atop the greens; but as they cook, the greens will wilt. (Alternatively, place the leaves in a large colander and pour boiling water over until the greens are just wilted, then layer over stems and proceed as above.) Place in pre-heated oven and bake for 45 minutes to an hour. If potatoes start to brown too quickly, lightly cover with foil (do not seal or potatoes will steam and not stay crisp).

Zucchini

Serves: 8 Prep time: 15-20 minutes Cook time: 45 minutes

Ingredients:

5 to 8 zucchini, depending on the diameter, about 7 to 8 inches long
1 cup finely ground almonds
1 cup rice, rinsed
4 medium-size tomatoes, finely chopped
4 tbsp melted butter
1 large onion, finely chopped
4 cloves garlic, crushed
4 tbsp finely chopped parsley
2 tbsp finely chopped fresh coriander leaves
1 1/2 tsp salt
1 tsp pepper
1 tsp oregano
1/2 tsp allspice
l/8 tsp cayenne
2 cups tomato juice mixed with
1/2 tsp salt and 1/2 tsp pepper

How To Do It

Cut off stem ends of zucchini and reserve; core zucchini. (Corer can be purchased from Middle Eastern stores.) Set aside. Combine remaining ingredients, except the tomato juice, to make stuffing. Stuff zucchini, and then close with inverted stem ends. Arrange tightly in a saucepan, and then place inverted plate on top. Add tomato juice and enough water to cover plate; bring to boil. Cover saucepan, then cook over medium heat for 45 minutes or until stuffing is cooked. Serve hot.

Steamed Fish & Scalllions with Peanut Oil

Serves: 2

Ingredients

1 knob or finger of ginger
4-5 stalks of scallions
12-14 oz. (340-400g) flat fish filets
finely ground white pepper
sea salt
2 tbsp peanut oil
2 tsp soy sauce

How To Do It

1. Peel ginger and halve. Julienne half of the knob into fine slivers, and set aside. With the other half, slice in larger pieces (these are for steaming)
2. Wash and trim scallions. Cut each stalk into 2-inch pieces, then thinly slice lengthwise into fine slivers. Slice remaining stalks into 2-inch pieces, then halve again once lengthwise (these are for steaming).
3. Prepare a large pot or wok for steaming, adding about 1-1/2 inches of water, and placing a metal rack or bamboo steamer above the water line. Bring water to a boil over high heat while you prepare fish.
4. Rinse fish filet and pat dry. Lay filet on a non-metallic plate or a piece of waxed paper on the steamer. Sprinkle with sea salt, then scatter larger pieces of ginger and scallion over filet. Carefully place in steamer, and cover, turning heat down to medium high.
5. Steam undisturbed for at least 7 minutes, then check fish for doneness — it should flake at the thickest part. If not done, add some hot water to the pot, and steam for another 2-3 minutes and check again.
6. Meanwhile heat a small skillet over medium high heat. Add peanut oil, and heat until just beginning to smoke. Remove ginger and scallion pieces, and place fish on a serving plate. Sprinkle with finely ground white pepper, and fresh julienned ginger and scallions. Drizzle soy sauce over fish, then immediately top with sizzling peanut oil.

Desserts

Cinnamon Crusted Strawberry Flan

Serves: 6

Prep time: 20 minutes
Cook time: 15 minutes
Chill: 30 minutes

Ingredients

Crust
2/3 cup rolled oats
1/2 cup whole grain pastry flour
1 tablespoon sugar
1 teaspoon ground cinnamon
1/4 teaspoon baking soda
2 tablespoons canola oil
3 tablespoons fat-free plain yogurt
Filling
1/4 cup strawberry all-fruit spread
1/2 teaspoon vanilla extract
1 and 1/2 pints strawberries, hulled

How To Do It

1. To make the crust: Preheat the oven to 375°F. Coat a baking sheet with cooking spray. In a medium bowl, combine the oats, flour, sugar, cinnamon, and baking soda. Stir in the oil and 2 tablespoons of the yogurt to make a soft, slightly sticky dough. If the dough is too stiff, add the remaining 1 tablespoon yogurt. Place the dough on the prepared baking sheet and pat evenly into a 10" circle. If the dough sticks to your hands, coat them lightly with cooking spray.
2. Place a 9" cake pan on the dough and trace around it with a sharp knife. With your fingers, push up and pinch the dough around the outside of the circle to make a 9" circle with a rim 1/4" high. Bake for 15 minutes, or until firm and golden. Remove from the oven and set aside to cool. 3. To make the filling: Meanwhile, in a small microwaveable bowl, combine the all-fruit spread and vanilla extract. Microwave on high power for 10 to 15 seconds, or until melted.

Brush a generous tablespoon evenly over the cooled crust. Arrange the strawberries evenly over the crust. Brush the remaining spread evenly over the strawberries, making sure to get some of the spread between the strawberries to secure them. Refrigerate for at least 30 minutes, or until the spread has jelled.

Possible substitution: Since cherries are well known for treating gout naturally, you may want to try this recipe with canned cherries or fresh bing cherries.

Cheese Spiced-up Pie

Prep time: 30 minutes Cook time: 1 hour

Ingredients

2 pie crusts or pate brisees
Filling:
1 small tub (12oz, 340g) low-fat cottage cheese
Set a strainer over a bowl and drain cheese for at least 8 hours, or overnight, in refrigerator.

1 lb. fresh amaranth, cleaned
1 lb. fresh watercress, cleaned and trimmed(or use 2 lb. of your favorite greens:Kale, endive, dandelions, nettles, wild garlic (Baerlauch), mustard greens, etc.)
2-4 cloves garlic, minced
3 tbsp olive oil
sea salt

How To Do It

1. Cut greens into 2-in. (3cm) lengths. Heat wok over medium-high heat, swirl oil around edges and add garlic. Cook until just fragrant, do not brown. Remove garlic and add greens to pan. Season with salt, and continue to sauté over medium heat.
2. Cover and cook for 5-8 minutes, or until vegetables are bright green and just tender. Add garlic back and remove from heat. When cool enough to handle, squeeze gently to remove excess water. Set aside. This can be done up to 2 days in advance.

PRE-HEAT OVEN to 400F (200C)

4-8 oz. of feta cheese
2 large eggs
2 tsp dill weed
2 tsp oregano
1 tsp thyme
1/2 tsp chervil (optional)
1 cup fresh minced parsley

1 bunch green onions, chopped (about 1 cup, 150g)
sea salt and ground black pepper

Directions

1. Combine drained cottage and feta cheeses, eggs, herbs and green onions. Add drained, cooked greens, and sea salt and ground black pepper to taste (it will depend on the saltiness of the cheeses you use).
2. Roll out one pie crust and mound filling onto crust to within 1-inch (5cm) of the edge of the crust. Place second crust over filling and crimp bottom crust over the top. Brush with olive oil. (For Heart-shaped pies, divide each pie crust into fourths (you will have 8 quarter circles). Fold each quarter-circle down its center, and using scissors, cut out a heart shape. Repeat with other quarter-circles. Fill with about 1 cup filling for each heart, leaving about 1/2-inch edge. Cover with top heart crust, bring bottom crust over, and crimp. Brush with olive oil.
3. Bake on middle shelf of pre-heated oven for 10 minutes, then turn oven down to 350F/180C. Bake another 35 minutes or until crust is golden brown. (Heart-shaped pies, bake another 15-20 minutes, until golden brown.) Cool before slicing. Makes a wonderful meat-less meal with crusty bread and crisp white wine, or a vegetable accompaniment to a simple roast chicken or fish.

Cinnamon Carrot Pancakes

Serves: 8 Prep time: 10 minutes Cook time: 8 minutes

Ingredients

2 cup Complete Pancake Mix,
½ cup Brown Sugar, packed
1/3 cup Raisins, packed
1 ½ cup Water, tap
¾ cup Carrots, raw, shredded
Salt, 1 dash
½ tsp Cloves, ground,
2 tsp Cinnamon, ground,
½ tsp Nutmeg, ground,

How To Do It

Combine pancake mix and water. In a separate bowl, combine remaining ingredients. Gently fold in carrot mixture to pancake batter. Let rest 5 minutes. Pour approx. 1/4 cup of batter onto lightly greased griddle. Cook as with any other pancake.

Veggie Pie

Serves: 6-8 Prep time: 30 minutes Cook time: 20 minutes

Ingredients

2 pounds fresh made or frozen dough, thawed
4 cups shredded potatoes
2 cups grated carrots
1 large onion, finely chopped
1 small hot pepper, very finely chopped
2 cloves garlic, crushed
2 Tbsp. finely chopped fresh coriander leaves
2 Tbsp. melted butter
1 egg, beaten
1 tsp. salt
1 tsp. cumin
½ tsp. pepper

How To Do It

1. Prepare dough for pies, if not using frozen, then set aside. Make a filling by thoroughly combining all remaining ingredients, then set aside. Form dough into 20 balls and place them on a tray lightly dusted with flour. Cover with a damp cloth; allow to stand in a warm place for 30 minutes, then roll balls into 5 to 6 inch rounds.
2. Divide filling into 20 equal parts. Place one part of the filling on each round then fold dough over the filling and close by firmly pinching edges together into half moon or triangle shape. (Prepare pies immediately after mixing filling—if left too long, the filling becomes somewhat watery.)
3. Place pies on well-greased baking trays, then bake in a 400° F preheated oven for 20 minutes or until pies turn golden brown. Remove from the oven, then brush with olive oil. Serve hot or cold. Eaten just out of the oven, these pies are very delicious.

Cheddar Pie

Serves: 8

Ingredients

1½ to 2 pounds fresh made or frozen dough, thawed
l/8 tsp. cayenne
4 cups grated cheddar cheese
1 tsp. pepper
4 Tbsp. olive oil
2 large onions, finely chopped
1½ tsp. salt
2 tbsp finely chopped fresh coriander leaves

How To Do It

1. Make the dough for the pies. Set it aside. To make the filling you will need to mix all of the ingredients that are left and leave this to the side. Next, you will need to make 20 balls of dough that are equal in size. Place the dough balls on a flour dusted cookie sheet. Cover the dough balls with a damp cloth and allow to sit in a warm place for about half an hour. Roll the balls into 6 inch circles.
2. The filling needs to be divided into 20 equal parts. Place the filling (each 1/20) into the dough ball. Fold the ball over the top of the filling to form a pizza slice shape. Be sure to pinch the edges of the crust closed. The filling needs to be placed in the pies ASAP, otherwise the filling can begin to change consistency into a more watery filling.
3. Put the pies onto a grease cookie sheet and place into a preheated oven at 400F for 20 minutes. When the pies turn a light golden brown color they are done. You should lightly brush the tops of the pies with olive oil. A diet for people with gout might prove to be a bit challenging at times, but if you are able to be creative you can find and make recipes that are fitting to you and your taste buds.

Vanilla Apple Waffles

Serves: 9 Prep time: 10 minutes Cook time: 10 minutes

Ingredients

1-1/2 cups whole wheat flour
2/3 cup oat bran
1/3 cup ground flax seed 2 T. sugar
1 tsp. salt
1 tsp. cinnamon
4 tsp. baking powder
1/2 tsp. baking soda
4 eggs, separated
2-1/2 cups buttermilk
2 tsp. vanilla
2 T. oil
3-1/2 cups shredded apples

How To Do It

In a large bowl, combine dry ingredients. In another bowl, whisk together egg yolks, vanilla and buttermilk. Stir into flour mixture until smooth. Use whisk if necessary. Stir in oil and apples. Beat egg whites until soft peaks form. Stir into mixture. Bake in waffle iron according to manufacturer's directions. I use round waffle irons. Spread with a little butter if desired. Place in warm oven while baking the rest of the waffles. It makes 9-1/2 waffles for me using 2/3 cup batter for each one.

Sweet Potato Pie

Serves: 4 Prep time: 20 minutes Cook time: 1 hour

Ingredients

1 reduced-fat 9-inch piecrust, unbaked
3 egg whites (or egg substitute equal to 2 eggs)
3/4 cup sugar
1 teaspoon ground cinnamon
1/2 teaspoon salt
1/2 teaspoon ginger
1/4 teaspoon ground cloves
1/8 teaspoon allspice
2 cups canned sweet potatoes, mashed
1 cup skim milk

How To Do It

Preheat oven to 425 degrees. Set aside piecrust. (We couldn't find a reduced-fat piecrust, so we used a regular one.) Combine remaining ingredients in a medium mixing bowl. Blend with electric mixer until smooth. Pour into piecrust, and cook at 425 degrees for about 15 minutes. Reduce the temperature to 350 degrees, and continue baking for about 45 minutes or until a toothpick inserted in the center comes out clean. Remove pie from oven, cool, and then chill in refrigerator overnight or for at least 4 hours. Serve with ice cream or non-fat vanilla yogurt.

Poached Fish Pie

Ingredients

Mashed Potatoes
1.5 lb (675g) floury potato
Sea salt and fresh ground pepper
1/3 cup + 2 tbsp (100 ml) milk, room temperature
4 tbsp (55g) butter, room temperature pinch fresh nutmeg (about 3 passes on a grater)

How To Do It

1. Peel potatoes, cut in quarters, and place in steamer. Steam over medium-high steam for 15-20 minutes, or until cooked through. Place milk, butter, salt and pepper in large bowl. Transfer hot potatoes to bowl, season with salt and pepper, and immediately mash or whip to fluffy consistency.
2. Add nutmeg, if using, and stir to mix through. (Actually, when I make mashed potatoes for fish pie, I usually just mash the potatoes with a bit of sea salt and ground black pepper and a drizzle of olive oil because there is so much butter, milk and cream in the sauce, it is too rich for my blood. But for company or a special occasion, I'll splurge on the butter and milk in the potatoes too.)

Ingredients

Poach Fish

1.5-2lb. (675-900g) haddock, cod, wahoo, mahimahi, or other firm white fish, with skin
1-3/4 cup (425ml) whole or low-fat milk (don't recommend using non-fat)
½ onion, sliced
8-10 peppercorns
3-4 small bay leaves
sea salt and fresh ground pepper

How To Do It

1. Pre-heat oven to 350F/180C. In small oven-proof pan with deep sides, lay onion slices, peppercorns and bay leaves in pan. Place fish, skin side up (this is supposed to further protect your fish from drying out) on top of onions.
2. Pour milk over fish, season with salt, and cover with parchment or wax paper. Cook in preheated oven for 15-20 minutes, or until fish is opaque (cooked through). Cooking time will depend on thickness of fish. Remove fish from pan,

and keep covered to retain heat. Strain milk to remove solids, **but KEEP MILK** to make Bechamel Sauce.

Ingredients

Make Bechamel Sauce
2 tbsp (30g) unsalted butter
1/3 cup (30g) flour
Reserved Milk from Poached Fish
2 tbsp heavy cream (or double cream)

How To Do It

Melt butter in saucepan, and immediately add flour. Stirring constantly, cook together for one minute. Add 2 tbsp of Reserved Milk, and whisk until milk is completely absorbed. Add 2 more tbsp of Reserved Milk, and stir to incorporate. Continue to add increasing amounts of milk to slurry in pan, and whisk well. Bring sauce slowly to a boil over medium heat, then add cream and remove from heat. Taste, and season with salt and pepper.

Ingredients

Assemble and Bake
5 large hard-boiled eggs, peeled
Small bunch of flat-leaf parsley, minced (about 2 tbsp)

How To Do It

1. Place 6-cup oven-proof casserole on baking sheet. Flake fish in large chunks into casserole. Add eggs, if using, or vegetables. Sprinkle with parsley. Pour hot sauce over all. Spread a layer of mashed potatoes over fish and, using a fork, make a traditional criss-cross pattern over the top. Drizzle with olive oil, and place casserole on baking sheet into middle shelf in oven.
2. Bake for 10 minutes, or until filling is hot throughout. Test filling with metal needle or skewer to make certain it is hot. If potatoes start to brown before filling is properly heated, cover lightly with foil/aluminium. If you're baking a pie that was begun 24 hours earlier and refrigerated: Cover with foil/aluminium and bake for 30 minutes. Test filling as outlined above. Remove foil and continue baking another 10 minutes or until potatoes lightly brown.

Mango-Filled French Toast

Ingredients

Fruit from 1-3 fully ripe mango

How To Do It

You can mash or dice the mango, especially if it shows any signs of being stringy. I left it in slices because this particular mango cut like butter anyway, and we like the texture of the fruit this way. Pre-heat oven to 400F (200C). A countertop or large toaster oven is perfect for a 2-person serving.

Ingredients

2 large or 3 medium eggs
1/2 cup (120ml) almond milk (or soy or low-fat milk)
1/2 tsp vanilla extract
1 tsp raw sugar
4 slices of whole wheat bread
Beat together eggs, milk, vanilla and sugar. Dip each side of bread in this mixture, then leave bread to soak up remaining milk while you prepare the topping.

Topping

1 slice of bread
1/4 cup (40g) macadamia nuts, chopped
2 tbsp raw sugar
Process bread, nuts and sugar in small bowl of food processor or blender.

To assemble

2 tbsp (30g) unsalted butter, melted
2 tsp raw sugar, or to taste

How To Do It

Butter a small baking dish. Lay 2 slices of soaked bread on the bottom. Top with mango slices (dice, or puree). Sprinkle fruit with 1 tsp. of raw sugar. Top with second slice of bread. Liberally sprinkle bread-nut topping, then drizzle with melted butter. Bake in pre-heated oven for 5 minutes, then turn oven down to 325F (for another 25 minutes). If top starts to brown to quickly, cover with foil to protect crust.

Drinks

Cherry Chilled Milk Shake

Serves: 1 Prep time: 5 minutes Cook time: 5 minutes

Ingredients

½ cup Yogurt cherry
½ Banana
1 cup Pitted cherries
¼ tablespoon *Fruit Advantage Cherry Juice Concentrate*
½ cup Milk (soy, 2% or low fat),

How To Do It

Take all the ingredients in a bowl, put them in a blender and blend until smooth, for about 1 – 2 minutes, on high speed. If the smoothie seems to thicken, you can add a couple of ice cubes to it. But do not add too many, as the smoothie can lose its taste if it becomes too watery. Make your cherry smoothie more attractive; add a drop of red food coloring.

Manana Smoothie

Serves: 2 Prep time: 10 minutes

Ingredients

1 cup 8th Continent Light Vanilla Soy Milk
1 cup Yogurt, Yoplait Light Very Vanilla, Fat Free
1 Banana, fresh, 1 medium
140 grams Dole Frozen Mango Chunks
.5 cup Bear Naked Fit Vanilla Almond Crunch
4 tbsp Kretschmer Original Toasted Wheat Germ

How To Do It

Add soy milk and yogurt to blender first. Add all other ingredients and blend to desired consistency.

Cucumber Yogurt Shake

Serves: 4-6 Prep time: 10 minutes

Ingredients

2 cups plain low-fat yogurt
1 medium cucumber (6 to 8 inches), peeled, quartered, then thinly sliced
2 Tbsp. finely chopped fresh mint
2 cloves garlic, crushed
½ tsp. salt

How To Do It Place all ingredients, except crushed ice and mint leaves, in a blender and blend for a minute. Serve with crushed ice and garnished with mint leaves or refrigerate for later use.

Salads

Vanilla Yogurt Tortellini

Serves: 20 Prep time: 15 minutes

Ingredients

5 Cups Cheese Tortellini
2 Cups Red Grapes
2 Cups Green Grapes
2 11oz cans Mandarin Oranges
1 cup Honey Mustard Dressing
6 oz Vanilla Yogurt
1.5 Cups Walnuts

How To Do It

Cook Tortellini by package directions and chill. Mix all ingredients. Top with Walnuts

Tomato and Mac Salad

Serves: 6 Prep time: 10 minutes

Ingredients

4 medium tomatoes, diced into
½-inch cubes
3 cups cooked macaroni
½ cup finely chopped fresh basil
2 cloves garlic, crushed
4 tbsp olive oil
2 tbsp vinegar
¾ tsp salt
½ tsp pepper

How To Do It

In a salad bowl, combine tomatoes, macaroni, and basil; set aside. Combine remaining ingredients then pour over tomato and macaroni mixture in salad bowl. Toss, chill, and serve.

Olives & Egg Salad

Serves: 16 Prep time: 30 minutes

Ingredients

1 large head cauliflower
1 large bunch broccoli
1 small onion (or 4 green ones)
1 pkg frozen peas (or pea pods)
2 cups mayo
1 cup low fat sour cream
1 tsp garlic powder

How To Do It

Mix mayo, sour cream and garlic powder in a small bowl. Break cauliflower and broccoli into bite sized pieces. Add onion. Toss sauce with broccoli, cauliflower and onion. Add peas last (if using pods, cut into 1/4 inch pieces. Refrigerate at least 4 hours or overnight.

Chicken Taco Salad

Serves: 6 Prep time: 20 minutes

Ingredients

Chicken breast—boil, then shred with fork
Olive Oil
Cumin Chilli Powder
1 Can Rotel tomatoes with green chillies
1 Large yellow onion, diced
1 Head Iceberg lettuce
1 Can black olives
Shredded low fat cheddar cheese
Low fat Sour Cream Guacamole (optional)

Homemade Salsa

1 large can peeled tomatoes
1 small bunch cilantro
1 medium/large oniongarlic salt to taste

How To Do It

In a large skillet, pour about 2 tbsp olive oil and turn up tomed/high heat. Sauté about 1/4 of the onions. Add the shredded chicken, cumin and chilli powder and Rotel. Simmer for approximately 20 minutes, stirring occasionally. Meanwhile, shred lettuce and place in bowls. When Chicken mixture is done, place a heaping on top of the lettuce and cover with cheese, olives, low fats our cream, the remaining onions. Combine salsa ingredients in blender. Add to salad... this will be used as your dressing.

Cole Slaw Classic

Serves: 8 Prep time: 20 minutes

Ingredients

2/3 cup vinegar
1/2 cup low fat whipping cream
2 large eggs, lightly beaten
1/4-1/2 cup Splenda
Pinch of salt
1 1/2 tbsp butter cut into pieces
1 (2-pound) head cabbage, shredded

How To Do It

Combine first 5 ingredients in a small, heavy saucepan; cook over low heat, stirring constantly with a wire whisk, 8 to 10 minutes or until thickened (mixture will appear curdled until it thickens). Remove from heat. Add butter, stirring until it melts. Pour over cabbage; toss gently to coat. Cover and chill. You can add 1/2 cup chopped walnuts and only raise the carb count by 1/2 gram. If you're on maintenance, 1/2 cup dried, chopped cranberries and the walnuts brings you in at a little under 10 grams.

Cranberry and Orange Salad

Serves: 8 Prep time: 20 minutes

Ingredients

Can crushed unsweetened pineapple (9-oz.)juice
1 package sugar-free cherry gelatin – (.3-oz.) tbsp lemon juice
1/4 cup artificial sweetener
1 cup fresh cranberries, chopped fine
1 small orange, peeled, quartered and chopped small
1 cup celery, chopped
1/2 cup pecans – or other nuts, optional

How To Do It

Drain pineapple and save juice. Set pineapple aside for later use. Combine pineapple juice with water to equal 2 cups liquid. Prepare gelatin according to package label using juice-water mixture for the liquid. Once gelatin is dissolved, stir in lemon juice. Chill until partially set. In a separate bowl, combine the pineapple, sugar substitute, cranberries, orange, celery and nuts. Add this mixture to the partially set gelatin and stir until blended. Pour into large mold or individual molds. Chill until firm. Do not use fresh or frozen pineapple in this recipe! It will not allow the gelatin to jell.

Dijon Mustard Vinaigrette

Ingredients

3 tbsp red wine vinegar
2 tbsp water
1 tbsp olive oil
1 tsp olive oil
1 tsp Dijon mustard
1/4 tbsp garlic powder

How To Do It

Combine all in a bowl. Blend well with a whisk. Chill overnight to blend flavors.

Cole Slaw

Serves: 3-5 Prep time: 10 minutes

Ingredients

Raw cabbage (shredded)
Mayonnaise
White distilled vinegar
Salt & pepper (to taste)

How To Do It

Per 1 cup of shredded cabbage mix the following: 2 tablespoons of mayonnaise ,2 teaspoons of vinegar, salt & pepper to taste

Eggplant Salad with Tomato Sauce

Serves: 2 Prep time: 15 minutes

Ingredients

1 large eggplant, cut 1/2" pieces
1 large onion, cut 1/2" pieces
1 can pitted black olives, diced small
1 small jar Spanish olives, diced into small pieces
1/4 cup cider vinegar, more to taste
1 quart tomato sauce

How To Do It

Mix all chopped ingredients and add the vinegar. Toss well to mix the vinegar with the mixed veggies. Let set a few minutes and toss again. Add the tomato sauce and mix again. Add red pepper and black to taste (1/2 tsp red is hot) Mix one more time before placing in a 4 qt. Corning ware pot. Bake in the oven at 325`F for about 1 hour (1 1/2 hours is mushy) Let cool to room temperature, toss and refrigerate before serving.

French Dressing

Serves: 4 Prep time: 15 minutes

Ingredients

1/2 cup salad oil
1/3 cup red wine vinegar
1 tbsp lemon juice
1 tsp Worcestershire sauce
1/2 tsp salt
1/4 package artificial sweetener, to taste
1/2 tsp dry mustard
1/2 tsp pepper
1 clove garlic, minced

How To Do It Put everything in a jar with screw on lid and shake well. Makes about 1cup

French Dressing Duex

Serves: 4-6
Prep time: 5 minutes

Ingredients

1/2 cup Walden farms ketchup
1/2 cup oil (canola or vegetable)
1/4 cup white vinegar
1 packet equal
1 tsp lemon juice
Dash of pepper

How To Do It

Stir all ingredients until combined

Chunky Chicken Salad

Serves: 4-6
Prep time: 15 minutes

Ingredients

1/4 cup soy sauce
1/4 cup olive oil
2 pounds skinless boneless chicken breast, cut in bite size chunks
Garlic powder, to taste
2 cups lettuce
1 large tomato
1medium cucumber
1/2 red onion black pepper, to taste
Balsamic vinegar, to taste

How To Do It

Heat oil in non-stick fry pan and sauté chicken with garlic powder until it turns a golden brown. Add soy sauce. Simmer on low heat for about 5 to 10 minutes. The oil will float a little to the top. That's okay. Make salad with the remaining items. Sprinkle with black pepper. NO SALT! That's what the soy sauce is for. When salad is ready, pour the hot mixture of chicken, oil and soy onto the salad. Add balsamic vinegar to taste and toss. The lettuce will wilt a little. You will love it!

Cranberry Jell-O Salad

Serves: 8
Prep time: 15 minutes

Ingredients

2 1/2 cups Diet Iced Botanicals (Cranberry-Raspberry)
1 large package Cranberry Jell-O
1/2 cup chopped celery
1/2 cup chopped pecans
1 1/2 cups cottage cheese
1/8 cup mayonnaise

How To Do It

Bring Botanicals to boil. Stir in Jell-O until dissolved. Chill until partially set (thickened – but not solid Pour 1/2 in8x8x2 inch glass pan. Stir 1/2 cup celery &1/2 cup nuts into pan—add additional celery& nuts to remaining Jell-O. Chill 8x8 pan & remaining Jell-O mixture---until Jell-O is firm. Mix together cottage cheese& Mayo---place on top of 8x8 layer of Jell-O. Take remaining Jell-O (if it is firm warm slightly in microwave & pour over cottage cheese).Chill until firm.

Spicy-Chicken Caesar Salad

Serves: 4
Prep time: 10 minutes

Ingredients

1 large chicken breast
Cajun spice or cayenne pepper to taste
2 tablespoons Hot Sauce
2 Cups romaine lettuce
2 tablespoons Caesar dressing
2 tablespoons parmesan cheese

How To Do It

Sprinkle spices on chicken breast. May be grill on the BBQ, baked, fried, etc. Cut in to 1 inch cubes and toss with hot sauce. Set aside. Mix lettuce, dressing and cheese. Put on a plate and top with chicken. Top with additional parmesan cheese if desired. I like mine really hot and spicy so I use cayenne Cajun spice will make it a little milder.

Fancy Pea Toss

Serves: 4-6 Prep time: 10 minutes

Ingredients

2 cups peas, canned – fancy
1 1/2 cups finely chopped onion
1 cup celery, chopped
2 cups lettuce, cut bite-sized
1 cup mayonnaise
10 slices bacon, cooked and crumbled
1/4 cup Parmesan cheese

How To Do It

Toss peas, onion, celery, and lettuce with mayonnaise in a serving bowl. Sprinkle bacon on top. Sprinkle with Parmesan cheese. Cover; refrigerate overnight. Little peas, celery, and bacon add crunch and color to this salad. It's a very nice change of pace for a picnic or potluck. Note that you can use frozen peas, if you prefer. You can use whatever variety of lettuce suits your taste.

Easy Honey Mustard

Serves: 1
Prep time: 5 minutes

Ingredients

1 tbsp Dijion Mustard
1 tbsp Spicey Brown Mustard
2 tbsp low fat Heavy Whipping Cream
1 Packet Splenda

How To Do It
Mix all ingredients and serve! Originally, I thought this up as a dip for chicken, but it also makes the BEST salad dressing. If you've been missing honey mustard dressing

Ginger Salad Dressing

Serves: 6 Prep time: 5 minutes

Ingredients

1/4 cup chopped onion
1/4 cup peanut oil, wine vinegar
2 tablespoons water
1 tablespoon ginger root –chopped
1 tablespoon chopped celery
1 tablespoon soy sauce
11/2 teaspoons tomato paste
1 1/2 teaspoons Splenda
1 teaspoon lemon juice
1 Dash
Salt and pepper

How To Do It

Combine all ingredients in blender container or wok bowl of food processor fitted with steel knife; process until almost smooth. May be kept refrigerated up to one week.

Hot Turnip and Dill Salad

Serves: 4 Prep time: 15 minutes

Ingredients

1 cup mayonnaise
3 tablespoons white wine
2 teaspoons vinegar
1/2 cup bacon grease
1/2 teaspoon fresh dill
2 packages artificial sweetener, sweet n low
3/4teaspoon salt
1/8 teaspoon pepper bacon strips, crushed
2 teaspoons onion

How To Do It

Whisk all ingredients together. Makes about 2 cups. Use about1/4 to 1/2 cup per large turnip, boiled until soft. Add crushed bacon and 2 tablespoons onion sautéed in bacon grease.

Chili-Chinese Chicken Salad

Serves: 5 Prep time: 20 minutes

Ingredients

For two large salads:
2 chicken breast, cooked with desired seasoning
2 large bowls of lettuce
Tomatoes (optional)

note: for Gout diets keep the amount of tomatoes at minimum
Crumbled bacon (optional)
Hot peppers (optional)
Slivered almonds (optional)
Desired shredded cheese (Cheddar is excellent)

Dressing

1/2 cup oil
1/3 cup apple cider vinegar
1 tablespoon soy sauce (low sodium)
2 packets Equal
Splenda 1 Dash ginger
1 Dash pepper
1 Dash garlic salt

How To Do It

Bring ingredients of dressing to a boil in a pan and stir with a whisk. Once all the ingredients are well-blended, pour over salads.

Cauliflower Salad in Italian Dressing

Serves: 6 Prep time: 10 minutes

Ingredients

3 cups cauliflower
2 tablespoons diced green bell pepper
2 tablespoons diced onion
1/4 cup water
3 tablespoons Italian salad dressing
1/4 teaspoon salt
1/8 teaspoon oregano, dry
1/8 teaspoon basil, dry
1/8 teaspoon garlic powder

How To Do It

Combine all ingredients in pan. Cover and cook over medium heat, stirring once in a while till 'flower is tender crisp, about 10 minutes Chill thoroughly.

Lime Vinaigrette

Prep time: 5 minutes

Ingredients

2 tablespoons red wine vinegar
2 tablespoons lime juice
1/4 teaspoon black pepper
1/4 cup cilantro leaves
Whole 1 clove garlic
1 tablespoon egg substitute liquid – (or 1 egg yolk)
2 teaspoons prepared mustard
1/2 cup oil
1 pinch salt

How To Do It

Put everything but half the cilantro and all of the oil in a blender. Process until smooth. with the blender running, slowly pour in the oil until it's well blended. Chop the remaining cilantro very fine and stir into the dressing. The cilantro taste is very strong. Start with just 2T if you like. The vinaigrette is an excellent marinade for ribs or fish. If you like a stronger lime flavor (for marinades) add 1T lime zest to the blender as well.

Waldorf Salad (Low Carb)

Serves: 6 Prep time: 15 minutes

Ingredients

2 cups jicama, peeled and cubed
2 tablespoons lemon juice
1/2 cup strawberries cut into 1/4s
1/2 cup celery, sliced
1/2 cup mayonnaise, more or less to taste
2 packets Splenda
3 tablespoons slivered almonds
2 tablespoons blue cheese crumbled (optional)
4 cups romaine lettuce, shredded

How To Do It

Toss Jicama cubes with lemon juice and let sit 5 minutes. Mix in remaining ingredients. Refrigerate 30 minutes or more before serving. Divide lettuce among 4 plates and spoon 1/4 of the salad over the top of each.

Munchy Mushroom Salad

Serves: 4-6 Prep time: 15 minutes

Ingredients

1/2 cup kalamata olives
1/2 cup green olives
1/2 cup black olives
1/2 cup banana peppers, rings
2 ounces pimientos
1/2 cup mushrooms, cut into pieces
1/2s1 cup Italian salad dressing bottled
3 tablespoons lemon juice
1 teaspoon black pepper, freshly ground
2 cloves garlic, smashed
2 cups water
1/2 teaspoon salt

How To Do It

1. Use whole, pitted olives –or olive halves (not slices) depending on how you want to use the mix. Banana peppers can be mild or hot -your choice. Drain and rinse all ingredients. Bring water, salt and lemon juice to a boil. Add mushrooms and boil for 3 minutes.
2. Drain well.Warm salad dressing, garlic and pepper to a low simmer, then remove from heat and let cool while you assemble the rest. In a gallon size zipper bag, place olives, mushrooms pimento and peppers. When dressing has cooled slightly, pour into bag and seal. Marinate 2-3 days, turning bag occasionally Drain or use with the dressing over salads.

Lemon Dressing

Prep time: 5 minutes

Ingredients

2 teaspoons salt
4 teaspoons Splenda
1 dash pepper
1 dash Paprika
1 1/3 cups salad oil
8 tablespoons vinegar
8 teaspoons lemon juice
teaspoon grated lemon rind, zest

How To Do It

Combine all ingredients in a jar with a tight fitting lid and shake until well blended. Refrigerate.

Spring Salad

Serves: 2 -3
Prep time: 10 minutes

Ingredients

1 medium cucumber
1 large tomato
2 green onions
4 tablespoons low carb Italian salad dressing
2 teaspoons Splenda

How To Do It

Dice vegetables- slice green onion, combine in a small bowl, sprinkle dressing and Splenda over and add salt and pepper if desired. Gently stir to mix and coat all, and refrigerate for at least 2 hours or overnight. Suggestions: This is always better the next day. This recipe is awesome with a steak or chicken breast. The marinade is good on the meat as well.

Crunchy Sweet Chicken Salad

Serves: 4
Prep time: 20 minutes

Ingredients

8 ounces cooked chicken breast half, diced small
1 ounce slivered almonds
1/2 cup jicama, diced small
1/2 cup diced celery
1/2 cup diced onion
4 tablespoons mayonnaise
2 packets splenda packets
1 each salt and pepper, to taste

How To Do It

Put jicama and 2T water in a baggie with 1 packet Splenda and let sit at room temperature for 1 hour, turning bag occasionally to marinate. When ready to make, mix all ingredients well including liquid from jicama. Refrigerate at least 2-3 hours to blend flavors. *note:1/2 cup of diced strawberries can be used instead, but don't add them until ready to serve and fold in gently. Start with 1 pack of Splenda/sweetener added to the salad mixture and taste before adding more. You may not like it as sweet as I do.

Tapenade

Serves: 4
Prep Time: 10 minutes

Ingredients

1/2 cup kalamata olives
1 tsp capers
1/4 cup extra virgin olive oil
1 tbsp balsamic vinegar

Equipment Needed

Chef's knife cutting board, mortar & pestle, small bowl, measuring cups and spoons
1/4 to 1/2 tsp oregano
1/4 to 1/2 tsp rosemary
1 clove garlic 1/8
tsp black or white pepper

Hints: The vinaigrette should run slightly from the tapenade after it sits for a few seconds. Tapenade may be prepared a day in advance. Experiment with other herbs and types of acids to complement other foods such as fish or cold meats. Wine or cider vinegar may be substituted to reduce the carbohydrate by 0.5 g per serving.

How To Do It

Chop olives until pieces are 1/8" or less. Crush capers and garlic with knife blade and mince fine. Grind oregano and rosemary with mortar and pestle until powdered. Combine all ingredients in small bowl. Cover and chill for 2 hours. Serve over cold asparagus or thin sliced tomato or other cold cooked vegetables.

Yummy Curry-Glazed Cod Salad

Serves 2

Ingredients

For the Salad
7-8 oz. package of dried soba noodles, cooked al dente
1-2 cups prepared Sea Salad
1/4 cup julienned carrots, about 1/2 small carrot (optional)
1-2 tsp toasted sesame seeds
lemon quarters
Dressing
1/2 cup rice vinegar
2 tsp raw sugar (or less regular sugar)
pea-size dollop of wasabi paste
sea salt, to taste
ground white pepper, to taste

How To Do It

Whisk together Dressing ingredients. Pour over cooked soba noodles. Toss together with Sea Salad and carrots, if using. Squeeze lemon juice atop noodles. Sprinkle top with sesame seeds Fish Curry Spice Mix:

1 tbsp ground coriander
1 tsp ground cumin
1/2 tsp ground fennel
1/2 tsp ground turmeric
Combine spices and set aside.
2 4oz. skinless filets of cod, or other flaky white meat fish
1 tbsp lemon juice per filet
sea salt
ground white pepper

Directions

Sprinkle each side of the filets with lemon juice, then with the curry spice mix. Let marinate for 20 minutes. Pre-heat pan over medium high heat. Season fish with salt and pepper. Add oil to pan, and place white side of filet down on pan, and gently press to make full contact. Cook for 2 minutes, then turn over and gently press. Cook another 3-4 minutes, or until fish flakes under a fork. Meanwhile plate the noodles. Place hot filets on noodles and serve immediately.

Shades of Potato Salad

Ingredients

For the potatoes:
2.2 lb. (1kg) total of mixed red, Yukon gold, and Peruvian purple potatoes
2 cloves garlic, finely minced
2-4 tbsp olive oil
sea salt
ground black pepper

How To Do It

1. Wash potatoes well, including a soak in a solution of 1 tbsp white vinegar for every 2 qt. /litre clean water. Scrub, rinse and place whole, unpeeled potatoes in large steamer that can hold potatoes in single layer.
2. Cook over medium high steam until potatoes are easily pierced with a knife blade. You might have to remove smaller potatoes earlier so they do not become water-logged.
3. Combine minced garlic and oil. While potatoes are hot, cube them into 1/2-inch (1.5-2cm) cubes, place in large bowl, and dress with garlic oil. Season to taste with sea salt and ground black pepper. Allow to cool to room temperature.

To finish salad:

4 scallions (green onions), white and light green parts only
(save the dark green for garnish), sliced thin
1/2 cup feta, crumbled
1/2 cup capers, rinsed and drained
1 sprig of fresh dill (about 1/4 cup)
Juice of 1 lemon
When potatoes have cooled, add scallions, feta, capers, dill and lemon juice, and toss gently to combine. Taste and correct seasoning — it should be lemony and salty-tart from the cheese and capers. Serve at room temperature.

Sesame dressing

Ingredients

2-4 cloves garlic finely minced
3 tbsp Toasted (aka "dark) sesame oil
1 tbsp Raw sugar
1 tsp sea salt
2 tbsp mirin, sake, or sherry
1 tsp soy sauce
Sesame seeds for garnish (optional)

How To Do It

Mix together sugar, salt, mirin and soy sauce. Stir to dissolve sugar. Pour over cooked cress and garnish with sesame seeds. Watercress and vegetable tempura kamaboko top this ramen for an easy, nutritious one-bowl meal.

Watercress Salad

Ingredients

1 large bunch watercress, about 1lb (450g)
2-4 tbsp olive oil
2-5 cloves garlic, diced (optional)
sea salt (optional)

How To Do It

1. Trim hollow stems of watercress to about 1-inch (5cm) of the leafy parts. Wash thoroughly in clean water, and vinegar-water solution. Cut into 2-inch (10cm) lengths. Heat wok or other large pot just to smoking point. Add enough olive oil to coat wok/pot, then add garlic, if using, and let gently brown (about 10-15 seconds), then remove from pan.
2. Add watercress, and using 2 wooden spoons or spatulas, turn to coat with oil. Add more oil to the sides of the wok, if necessary, but not directly on the greens. Continue cooking on medium high to high heat until the cress wilts and becomes bright green. Remove from heat and add salt to taste, if using. Cover and leave in pan another 5 minutes. Gently squeeze greens to remove excess moisture, and either dress or use right away, or store in fridge for up to 3 days. If storing, be certain the greens will be cooked again. If using as a ramen topping or side dish, microwave briefly to heat through before serving.

Crispy Kale Salad

Serves: 6-10

Prep time: 5 minutes
Cook time: 12 minutes
1 bunch of kale (about 1 lb/450g)
A drizzle of olive oil — no more than 1 tbsp
sea salt

How To Do It

1. Remove the leaves from the stems. You can cut them off, but I prefer to tear them. Hold a branch with the stem side up, and gently (always gently) tear away bite size pieces of leaves from the branch. Spin or pat the leaves dry. Or air dry. Any method works, just as long as the leaves are completely dry before you continue. Preheat oven to 325 F/180C.
2. Place completely dry leaves on a large baking sheet (cookie sheet or jelly roll pan), and drizzle regular or light olive oil over the top. Massage — gently, of course — the oil through the pile of leaves, and then spread out on the pan. (You may need 2 pans or to do this in 2 batches for 1 lb. of kale.) Sprinkle with sea salt to taste (we use about a 1/4 teaspoon for each pan). Bake in preheated oven for 10-12 minutes, or until the leaves turn from jade green to dark forest green, and take on a translucent look. You'll notice the potato chip-like aroma emanating from your oven, too.

Gai Choy Salad

2 tbsp white vinegar and
2 quarts/liters cool water

How To Do It

1. To prepare mature gai choy for cooking, remove stems from core and wash well first in clean container of water, rubbing away the soil and grit at the bottom of the stems. Remove vegetables from water, drain water and fill container with a solution of 2 tbsp white vinegar and 2 quarts/liters cool water.
2. Rinse stems and leaves thoroughly in this solution. Lift out of water, swishing leaves gently as you lift. Rinse again with clean water. Drain in colander. Separate stems and leafy parts. Halve and julienne leafy greens; and halve and dice stems. If using for braised dishes or soups, add thick stem pieces early to cook down and leafy bits in the last 15-20 minutes of cooking.

Iceberg Salad

Serves: 1 Prep time: 8 minutes

Ingredients

Iceberg lettuce
Apple cider vinegar
4 strips bacon
Onions
Brown sugar
Sesame oil

How To Do It

Fry bacon very crisp, shred lettuce, dice or slice the onions warm 3-4 tablespoons sesame oil, crunch up bacon, put on lettuce and onions, twin brown sugar to taste, vinegar to taste.

Mushroom Salad in Italian Dressing

Serves: 2 Prep time: 5 minutes

Ingredients

3 tablespoons Italian salad dressing
1 tablespoon Parmesan cheese
2 cups sliced mushrooms thinly sliced

How To Do It

Mix dressing and cheese. Stir in the mushrooms. Chill several hours.

Pecans and Pineapples Too! Salad

Serves: 2 Prep time: 5 minutes

Ingredients

8 ounces low fat cream cheese
1/2 cup chopped pecans
1 cup diced celery
1 small can crushed pineapple
1 pkg. lime gelatine
1 3/4 cup hot water
1 pinch salt

How To Do It

Mash cream cheese. Blend in pineapple. Add nuts and celery. Dissolve gelatin in water. Cool. Mix with cream cheese mixture. Pour into mold or pan. Chill.

Snapper Salad

Serves: 4 Prep time: 5 minutes

Ingredients

2 cups romaine lettuce chopped
2 cups bok choy, chopped
1/2 cup endive, chopped
1/2 cup spinach stems removed and chopped
1/2 cup red cabbage, chopped
1/2 cup cucumbers, peeled and sliced
1/2 cup celery, sliced
1/2 cup mushrooms, sliced
1/4 cup carrot shreds

How To Do It

Toss everything together. The book suggests a poppy seed dressing, but I have not found one that was low-carb/low-sugar, so I usually use a good Italian dressing and it's a fine salad

Spinach Salad

Serves: 4 Prep Time: 10 minutes

Ingredients

1 Bunch of Spinach
6 fresh mushrooms
1 cup bean sprouts
2 strips turkey bacon
1 1/2 tbsp Renees Gourmet Dressing, Cucumber Dill flavour

How To Do It Wash and Chop spinach into bite size pieces, chop mushrooms, add bean sprouts, fry bacon till crisp, crumble and add. Mix in dressing.

Side Salad 2

Prep time: 10 minutes

Ingredients

1/4 pound salami, hard cut 1/2" thick
1/2 pound mozzarella cheese, cubed
1 cup grape tomatoes, halved
1/8 cup fresh basil, chopped fine
1/4 cup olive oil, light salt and pepper

How To Do It

Toss together. Serve with diet flat bread grilled with olive oil and garlic salt.

Sesame Seed Oriental Dressing

Prep time: 5 minutes

Ingredients

1 tbsp Sesame Seed Oil
2 tbsp Canola Oil
1 tsp Sesame Seeds
1 tsp Splenda
1 tbsp apple cider vinegar
Salt & pepper to taste

How To Do It

Mix all ingredients in a 1/2 cup measuring cup.

Simple Salad

Prep time: 15 minutes

Ingredients

12 cherry tomatoes, cut in half
1 large cucumber, wash and slice about 1/4" slices
1 small red onion, cut into thin slices and separate into rings
6 green olives, w/pimento cut into 1/2s (optional)
1 lemon cut in 1/2 and slice very thin –make sure peel is clean
2 tablespoons fresh parsley, chopped (2 to 3)
1/3 cup bottled Italian or Caesar dressing, salt and pepper to taste

How To Do It

Toss everything together and let marinate in the refrigerator for an hour before serving. By itself or this is also excellent spooned over some lettuce, cabbage or fresh spinach.

Lettuce Mix Salad

Prep time: 15

Ingredients

Good sized handful of spring greens lettuce mix. Hidden valley ranch dressing package mixed with sour cream instead of mayo (much better that way). Mix a little water and/or cream to get a more fluid consistency.1 Safeway Select brand Chicken, Parmesan, Mushroom, and Spinach Sausage, sautéed whole (slice when cooked), or any brand that has no carbs/sugar. A small sprinkling of Planter's mixed salted nuts instead of croutons (more natural and yummier than store bought croutons).

How To Do It

Toss all ingredients in a salad bowl with a tablespoon or two of your dressing, and you'll have the most amazing brunch, lunch or dinner. Add a sprinkling of garlic powder and pepper for extra zip).

Sweet Orange Marinade

Prep time: 5 minutes

Ingredients

1/2 cup oil, grape seed or olive or vegetable
3 packets sweetener
2 tablespoons grated orange peel
4 tablespoons red wine vinegar
1 teaspoon orange extract
2 tablespoons chopped parsley
1 tablespoon red bell pepper, diced very fine
1 tablespoon green bell pepper, diced very fine

How To Do It

Put the vinegar, sweetener, extract, and 1T orange peel into a blender and blend. Slowly blend in the oil. Stir in the remaining ingredients. Refrigerate, tightly covered.

This is a good marinade for chicken, fish or pork and makes and excellent dressing for spinach salad.

Island Salad Dressing

Prep time: 5 minutes

Ingredients

1 tablespoon mayonnaise
2 teaspoons sugar free ketchup
2 teaspoons apple cider vinegar
1/2 teaspoon Worcestershire sauce
1 Dash garlic powder
2 teaspoons sweet relish

How To Do It

Mix all together and chill before serving

Tuna & Goat Cheese Caesar Salad

Serves: 1
Prep time: 8 minutes

Ingredients

1/4 cup tuna, canned
1/4 cup crumbled goat cheese (can buy at grocery store)
2 cups lettuce
2 tablespoons Caesar dressing

How To Do It

Mix all ingredients! Only 210 calories, 13 grams of fat, 22 grams of protein and 4 grams of carbs... delicious!

Tuna Cheese Salad

Serves: 2
Prep time: 10 minutes

Ingredients

2 cans of tuna packed in vegetable oil
Minced onion as desired
Minced celery as desired
Cheddar Cheese as desired
Chopped bacon as desired
Mayo as desired
2 tbsp Balsamic Vinegar

How To Do It

Prepare everything but tuna, mayo, and balsamic in a large bowl. Add as much mayo as you'd like. Add the tuna. Mix until all ingredients are well mixed and until the tuna is the consistency that you like. Add the balsamic. Mix until balsamic is evenly spread throughout the tuna, or until all the tuna has a slight brown tint to it from the balsamic. Put fork into tuna, lift fork to mouth, enjoy.

Soups

Creamy Carrot and Turnip Soup

Serves: 2
Prep time: 5 minutes
Cook time: 9 minutes

Ingredients

Boil a large fowl
3 quarts water
1 teacupful rice
1 carrot, sliced
1 turnip, sliced
1 celery, small piece
1 onion
2 tbsp. of butter
1 tbsp of flour
1 cinnamon, small piece
1 mace, small piece
4 whole cloves
1 1/2 tbsp salt
1/4 tsp pepper
Pint of cream

How To Do It

1. Boil a large fowl in three quarts of water until tender (the water should never more than bubble). Skim off the fat, and add a teacupful of rice, and, also, a slice of carrot, one of turnip, a small piece of celery and an onion, which have been cooked slowly for fifteen minutes in two large table-spoonfuls of butter. Skim this butter carefully from the vegetables, and into the pan in which it is, stir a table-spoonful of flour.
2. Cook until smooth, but not brown. Add this, as well as a small piece of cinnamon and of mace, and four whole cloves. Cook all together slowly for two hours. Chop and pound the breast of the fowl very fine. Rub the soup through a fine sieve; add the pounded breast and again rub the whole through the sieve. Put back on the fire and add one and a half table-spoonfuls of salt, a fourth of a teaspoonful of pepper and a pint of cream, which has come just to a boil. Boil up once and serve. This is a delicious soup.

Chicken & Veal Soup

Serves: 2
Prep time: 5 minutes
Cook time: 9 minutes

Ingredients

1 Chicken weighing 3 pounds
3 pounds veal
2 large onions
2 carrots, large slices
4 celery, stalks
3 tbsp butter
1 tbsp curry powder
4 tbsp flour
Salt and pepper to taste
5 quarts water

How To Do It

1. Take two table-spoonfuls of the fat from the opening in the chicken and put in the soup pot As soon as melted, put in the vegetables, which have been cut very fine. Let all cook together for twenty minutes, stirring frequently, that it may not burn; then add the veal, cut into small pieces. Cook fifteen minutes longer; then add the whole chicken and the water. Cover, and let it come to a boil. Skim, and set back where it will simmer for four hours (in the mean time taking out the chicken when it is tender).
2. Now put the butter into a small frying-pan, and when hot, add the dry flour. Stir until a rich brown; then take from the fire and add the curry powder. Stir this mixture into the soup, and let it cook half an hour longer; then strain through a sieve, rinse out the soup pot and return the strained soup to it. Add salt and pepper and the chicken (which has been freed from the bones and skin and cut into small pieces); simmer very gently thirty minutes. Skim off any fat that may rise to the top, and serve. This soup is served with plain boiled rice in a separate dish or with small squares of fried or toasted bread. The rice can be served in the soup if you choose.

Perfect Pumpkin Soup

Serves: 2 Prep time: 5 minutes Cook time: 9 minutes

Ingredients

2 lbs pumpkin
1 1/2 pint boiling milk
Butter, size of an egg
1 tsp sugar
Salt and pepper to taste
3 slices of stale bread

How To Do It

Take out seeds and pare off the rind. Cut into small pieces, and put into a stew-pan with half a pint of water. Simmer slowly an hour and a half, then rub through a sieve and put back on the fire with one and a half pints of boiling milk, butter the size of an egg, one tea-spoonful of sugar, salt and pepper to taste, and three slices of stale bread, cut into small squares. Stir occasionally; and when it boils, serve.

Onion and Milk Soup

Serves: 2 Prep time: 5 minutes Cook time: 9 minutes

Ingredients

One quart milk
6 large onions
4 egg yolks
3 tbsp of butter
1 large tbsp flour
1 cup cream
Salt and pepper to taste

How To Do It

1. One quart of milk, six large onions, yolks of four eggs, three table-spoonfuls of butter, a large one of flour, one cupful of cream, salt, pepper. Put the butter in a frying-pan. Cut the onions into thin slices and drop in the butter. Stir until they begin to cook; then cover tight and set back where they will simmer, but not burn, for half an hour. Now put the milk on to boil, and then add the dry flour to the onions, and stir constantly for three minutes over the fire.
2. Then turn the mixture into the milk and cook fifteen minutes. Rub the soup through a strainer, return to the fire, season with salt and pepper. Beat the yokes of the eggs well; add the cream to them and stir into the soup. Cook three minutes, stirring constantly. If you have no cream, use milk, in which case add a table-spoonful of butter at the same time.

Asparagus Soup

Serves: 2
Prep time: 5 minutes
Cook time: 9 minutes

Ingredients

2 bundles of asparagus
One quart of white stock or water
1 pint milk
1 pint cream
3 tbsp butter
3 tbsp flour
1 onion
Salt and pepper to taste

How To Do It

1. Two bundles of asparagus, one quart of white stock or water, one pint of milk, and one of cream, if stock is used, but if water, use all cream; three table-spoonfuls of butter, three of flour, one onion, salt and pepper. Cut the tops from one bunch of the asparagus and cook them twenty minutes in salted water to cover. The remainder of the asparagus cook twenty minutes in the quart of stock or water.
2. Cut the onion into thin slices and fry in the butter ten minutes, being careful not to burn; then add the asparagus that has been boiled in the stock. Cook five minutes, stirring constantly; then add flour, and cook five minutes longer. Turn this mixture into the boiling stock and boil gently twenty minutes.
3. Rub through a sieve; add the milk and cream, which has just come to a boil, and also the asparagus heads. Season with salt and pepper, and serve. Dropped eggs can be served with it if you choose, but they are rattier heavy for such a delicate soup.

Ground Beef Soup

Serves: 2
Prep time: 5 minutes
Cook time: 9 minutes

Ingredients

1 pound ground beef
2 quarts water
2 small new carrots
1 pound beef bones
2 small potatoes
1 onion
1 tomato
Fresh or canned Parsley

How To Do It

1. Boil the beef, bones, and vegetables in two quarts of water over a slow fire—adding pepper and salt. Skim occasionally, and after two hours add two tablespoons of sherry; then strain through fine soup-strainer or cheese-cloth. This is the basis of all the following soups, except when otherwise stated.

2. To make this stock richer, add a turkey leg to above receipt; boil one and a half hours, then add one-half a pound of finely chopped beef. Cook for half an hour longer, then strain. To make meat jelly, add a little gelatine to the soup stock five minutes before straining.

3. To give a good dark color to the stock, add a few drops of "caramel," which is prepared in the following manner: Put three tablespoons of granulated sugar into a saucepan with a little water, and until the sugar has become dark and reddish; then add a little more water and boil again until the sugar is melted. Strain and pour into a bottle when the caramel will keep perfectly for several weeks. Note... be careful about how much you have of this soup, as too much meat isn't Gout Friendly, but a small amount is fine.

Codfish Treat Soup

Serves: 2
Prep time: 5 minutes
Cook time: 9 minutes

Ingredients

½ lb salt codfish
4 tbsp of good olive-oil
1 small onion
Bunch of parsley stems
1 small piece of celery
1 bay-leaf
Small sprig of thyme
2 tomatoes
2 tbsp dry white wine
1 medium-sized potato
1 cup of water
Salt and paper
Toasted or fried bread

How To Do It

1. Take one-half pound of salt codfish that has been soaked, cut it up into squares, but not small. Prepare in a saucepan four tablespoons of good olive-oil, and one small onion cut into pieces. Cook the onion in the oil over a slow fire, without allowing the onion to become colored, and then add a small bunch of parsley stems, a small piece of celery, a bay-leaf, and a small sprig of thyme.
2. Cool for a few moments, then add two tomatoes, skinned and with the seeds removed, and cut into slices, two tablespoons of dry white wine, and one medium-sized potato, peeled and cut into slices, and, lastly, one cup of water. When the potato is half cooked, add the codfish, then one-half tablespoon more of olive-oil. Remove the parsley stems, and put in instead one-half tablespoon of chopped-up parsley; add a good pinch of pepper, and some salt, if needed. When the vegetables are thoroughly cooked pour the soup over pieces of toasted or fried bread, and serve.

Everything-in Vegetable soup

Serves: 2
Prep time: 5 minutes
Cook time: 9 minutes

Ingredients

Cabbage
Carrots
Celery
Onions
Turnips
Lettuce
Squash
Potatoes
Beans
Peas
1 heaping tbsp butter
Salt and pepper
1 tbsp tomato paste
1/3 cup hot water
Slice of bread

How To Do It

1. Take some cabbage, carrots, celery, onions, turnips, lettuce, squash, potatoes, beans, and peas. Chop each into very small pieces, wash and drain. Take a saucepan, put in a heaping tablespoon of butter; chop up another small piece of onion and add to butter and fry until onion is golden; then add all the vegetables, salt, and pepper, and cover the saucepan.
2. When the vegetables are half cooked, and their juice has become absorbed, dissolve one tablespoon of tomato paste in one-third of a cup of hot water, and add. Instead of the tomato paste there may be added to the onion, before putting in the vegetables, one tomato, peeled and cut into small pieces.
3. When the tomato is cooked add the vegetables. Then add water, a little at a time, until you have sufficient quantity for two persons. Take a slice of bread and cut into small squares or diamonds—toast or fry as desired—put these into the soup plates, and pour the soup (without straining) over them.

Chicken Soup for your Gout

Ingredients

The Broth:

2 stewing/soup hens (about 3 lbs/1.5 kg, total weight)
OR 5-6 lbs (2.5-3kg) assorted fresh chicken bones from your butcher
OR 1 whole chicken fryer (3-3.5 lb/1.5-2kg)
1 hand of ginger, scrubbed well and sliced lengthwise (peeling is optional)
1 lb. carrots, scrubbed well and trimmed
1 medium onion, scrubbed well and dark brown layers removed, halved lengthwise

How To Do It

1. The critical factor in broth-making is, of course, the bones for flavor, the skin for flavor and unctuousness, and the joints/tendons for body. You can make soup with fresh chicken carcasses alone, but not with just meat alone. Place chicken/bones, ginger, carrots and onion in 6-7 quart slow-cooker, and cover with water. Set on HIGH for at least 3 hours or until the mixture comes to a boil. Remove any "scum" that rises to the surface. Turn slow-cooker setting to LOW, and leave forat least 8 hours. Turn off slow-cooker and carefully remove the chicken and all solids to a colander placed in a large soup pot. Debone chicken and keep meat in separate container in fridge. Strain broth through a sieve into the same pot or pan into which the broth solids earlier drained. When broth reaches room temperature, place in a tightly covered container to store in fridge overnight. Remove most (85%) of fat layer from the chilled broth, then return to soup pot or Dutch oven. Add diced chicken meat, 2 cups water and bring to rolling boil for at least 10 minutes before adding other ingredients. To Finish Soup: Add 3-4 lbs (1.5-2kg) of diced vegetables and/or shredded leaf greens as you like or according to what is in season. I try to get as many colors of the rainbow as possible into the pot, each providing important nutrients and vitamins:
2. Add root and other longer-cooking vegetables early on. Save leafy greens and vegetables that turn to mush (e.g., potatoes, cooked beans like red kidney or black beans, and hard squashes like kabocha) for the last 30 minutes of cooking. Add 2 cups of fully cooked small pasta shapes (optional).
3. Add seasoning to taste: sea salt, ground black pepper, and up to 1-1/2 tsp. of chervil, or herb of your choice: fresh oregano, marjoram, savoury (especially nice if soup includes beans), thyme, basil. Simmer on medium-low until vegetables are tender and cooked through, about 30 minutes to 1 hour, depending on what vegetables you add. Taste again to correct seasoning. Serve hot, with bread

Beans Beans Beans! Soup

Serves: 6 Prep time: 15 minutes Cook time: 35 minutes

Ingredients

5 cups vegetable or chicken broth
1 can (14.5 ounces) Italian stewed tomatoes
1 can (19 ounces) red kidney beans, rinsed and drained
1 can (19 ounces) pinto beans, rinsed and drained
2 onions, chopped
3 cloves garlic, minced
2 teaspoons dried rosemary
1 teaspoon dried oregano
1 teaspoon dried savoury
1/2 teaspoon freshly ground black pepper
1/4 teaspoon salt
1 turnip, peeled and cut into 1/2 inch pieces
2 cups cut green beans

How To Do It

Place the broth, tomatoes (with juice), kidney beans, pinto beans, onions, garlic, rosemary, oregano, savoury, pepper, and salt in a large saucepan. Bring to a boil over high heat. Reduce the heat to low, cover, and simmer for 20 minutes, stirring occasionally. Add the green beans and turnip. Simmer, covered, for 15 minutes, or until the turnip is tender.

Resources:

YumsUp.com

- Step-by-step recipes videos to make great tasting recipes for every meal of the day.

- **Website:** YumsUp.com

Traverse Bay Farms

- Michigan-grown tart cherry juice and cherry capsule to reduce uric acid naturally. Cherries are an excellent natural way to remove excessive uric acid from the body.

- Winner of 30+ national food awards at America's largest and most competitive food competitions. #1 nationally award-winning superfood company in America.

Complete selection of all national salsa, fruit-based barbecue sauces, jams, jellies and more. Chocolate-covered dried cherries, strawberries, blueberries and more. Cherry juice concentrate to healthy joints and more. If you're looking for all-natural products, check out Traverse Bay Farms.

- **Website:** TraverseBayFarms.com

Health Smart Recipes

- How-to Recipes and Information.

- **Website:** HealthSmartRecipes.com

Disclaimer: The purpose of the recipes in this book are to support a gout friendly lifestyle. The author of the book does not take ownership of the recipes in this book. Use the information in this book to enjoy a gout free lifestyle.

Made in United States
Troutdale, OR
06/02/2024

20273256R00060